BEATING ABOUT THE BUSH

The Idiot's Guide to Bird Watching

BEATING
about
THE BUSH

The Idiot's Guide to Bird Watching

Kenneth Newman

Cartoons by Dr Jack

SOUTHERN
BOOK PUBLISHERS

ISBN 1 86812 442 8

First edition, first impression 1992

Published by
Southern Book Publishers (Pty) Ltd
P O Box 3103, Halfway House, 1685

Cover illustration by Dr Jack

Illustrations by Kenneth Newman

Cartoons by Dr Jack

Book design & typography
by Richard Collins
Set in 10 on 12 pt Palatino
by D&R Design cc, Pretoria

Repro by Remata Bureau & Printers, Midrand

Printed and bound by Creda Press, Cape Town

CONTENTS

PART I
AN INTRODUCTION TO BIRDING 1

PART II
HELPFUL NOTES ON SPECIFIC ID PROBLEMS 41

HOW TO USE THIS BOOK

There are two parts to this book: the first deals with general information about how to start birdwatching, where to find birds and what to look at when you do find them. The second part gives detailed information to help you distinguish between similar bird species.

Please note that page references are to *Newman's Birds of Southern Africa* unless specified otherwise. You will need to refer to the colour plates in *Newman's Birds* while reading Part 2 of this book.

PART I

An introduction
to birding

PART I An introduction to birding

WHY WATCH BIRDS?

People who don't look at birds often ask this question. The answer is that people who *do* look at birds do so because they are interested in and curious about wild things and derive pleasure from contacts with them. Presumably those who ask such a question have not developed this curiosity, although they may do so in time. When one has an interest in wild things it is birds, of all creatures, that are the most easily seen. They are conspicuous and are with us all the time, as close as the garden or the office window, and it costs nothing to see them.

Birds are elegant, highly active creatures that provide incalculable mental stimulation and joy to the watcher. The beauty of the more colourful species and the subtlety of tones in those that, at first glance, may appear sombre are infinitely more varied than in most other creatures with the sole exception, perhaps, of butterflies. In addition to the visual stimulation provided by birds there is also the pleasure that can be derived from their songs, some highly complex and beautiful in their rendering; an asset that even butterflies lack.

Birding combines mild outdoor exercise in pleasant surroundings with relaxed yet absorbing learning. It's also something that can be combined with photography for those with an itchy camera finger, especially when bird-watching from a motor car in wildlife reserves. In fact an interest in birds makes visits to game reserves infinitely more rewarding and is a refreshing deviation from seeking the 'big five'. Bird-watching can be done anywhere and at any time, alone, with a friend or in a group.

There are various degrees of competence to which the novice bird-watcher can aspire. Many people simply look at birds from their window or feed them in the garden and derive pleasure merely from becoming familiar with them and being able to name a few. Others take it a little further and note the birds seen during walks, or take walks in specific places where birds are

The weekend twitcher

known to be plentiful. Many join a bird club as a way of meeting other birders, sharing their experiences and learning from the more knowledgeable members. Joining a bird club also enables one to visit birding places that might otherwise be unknown or closed to the general public, and to enjoy evening lectures and film shows about birds.

Many of the more energetic bird-watchers keep monthly lists of the birds they have seen, or keep a record of the various species recorded in their gardens. Others like to record birds seen in a specific region, and may even take part in a bird census organised by a bird club. Another approach to bird-watching is the compilation of a life list, the tallying of every kind of bird seen in one's lifetime; it encourages a lot of friendly rivalry. Finally there are those who make bird-watching an obsession. They are called 'twitchers'. A twitcher must personally see every new bird recorded in the country, and often in other countries too. To this end he or she will rush from one corner of the land to the other, often at great expense, in order to 'twitch' rare or vagrant species that other 'lesser birders' will not have seen. The important rule in twitching is to stay ahead of the *hoi polloi*. Any twitcher whose life list does not reach four figures has hardly made the grade. I am not a twitcher.

WHO WATCHES BIRDS?

Organised bird-watching in southern Africa started in 1930 with the formation of the (then) South African Ornithological Society, now known as the Southern African Ornithological Society or SAOS. In its early years SAOS membership comprised mostly scientists, but following the Second World War more and more amateur bird-watchers joined. Today the majority of SAOS members are non-professional bird-watchers, and they become members by joining one of the local bird clubs, which are the branches of the SAOS. The Society has some 15 regional branches.

The great upsurge of interest in birds and bird-watching really began during the early 1980s, probably as a direct result of interest stimulated by books, films and TV programmes about birds written or presented by well-known personalities such as the late Sir Peter Scott, Richard Attenborough, Richard Burton and others. Today bird-watching, or birding as it is becoming increasingly known, is said to be the fastest growing free-time occupation. In Britain alone, where most bird-watchers are members of the Royal Society for the Protection of Birds (RSPB), the membership of that society soared from 20 000 in 1960 to 375 000 in 1984, and is higher still today. Similar increases have occurred in other countries. In considering these figures for society or club membership it must be remembered that many more bird-watchers do not join bird clubs or societies, preferring to go it alone.

In South Africa the increase in the number of bird-watchers has been no less dramatic in recent years. Bird identification courses organised by bird clubs or by independent individuals usually enjoy full houses while large business corporations themselves often organise bird-watching weekends for their clients. So who watches birds? Almost everyone.

HOW TO GO ABOUT IT

Fieldguides

The simple answer is to buy a good bird book (preferably mine of course) and a pair of binoculars. But in all seriousness there is a little more to it, and a few words of guidance will not be amiss.

In order to identify birds correctly it is necessary to have a book that illustrates each bird clearly, describes each one and provides a map of its distribution. The best of these books are fairly small and easy to carry. They are called fieldguides, and it is possible to buy special fieldguide carriers with shoulder straps for easier use in the field.

The type of fieldguide you choose will depend on the layout and style of illustration that most appeals to you. Some fieldguides use photographs to illustrate the birds, others use paintings. Even where good photographs are used this approach has its shortcomings in that each bird is usually illustrated by only one picture. Also, with some of the rarer or difficult to photograph birds the author often needs to rely on second-rate photographs or resort to a hand-painted one.

The advantage of hand-painted illustrations is that there is no limit to the number of pictures that can be used for each bird. Species that have different immature and adult plumages, and those that have plumage variations, can all be shown in addition to flight pictures where these are needed. Thus, in my own fieldguide *Newman's Birds of Southern Africa*, it has been possible in some instances to show as many as nine illustrations of one species (see Bateleur: p.161).

Another advantage of hand-painted illustrations is that birds can be consistently depicted in their most characteristic jizz (see the discussion about a bird's jizz on page 22 of this book), and their most useful field features highlighted, something not always possible in photographs. Also the artist is able to show each member of a bird family in the same characteristic jizz of that family and to highlight individual differences.

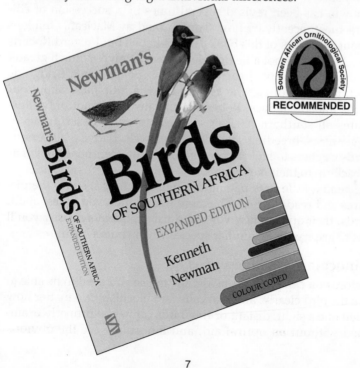

In a fieldguide it is essential that the descriptive text for each species be on the page opposite its illustration. In this way its seasonality, description, call and distribution can all be compared directly with the bird's picture. There is nothing quite so frustrating as to find that illustration and descriptive text are in different parts of the book.

While on the subject of fieldguides, both for beginners and experienced bird-watchers, I should emphasise that the purpose of a fieldguide is simply to depict the bird and to give a brief description of its various plumages and how they may differ from those of other, similar birds, plus a description of its call and where it may be found. If a fieldguide were to attempt to go beyond these simple identification clues for each species it would become too bulky and cumbersome for field use.

Having said all this I hasten to recommend a book that may be said to have been the forerunner of bird books in southern Africa, and I refer of course to the well-known, well-loved *Roberts' Birds of Southern Africa*, a tome from which I and a host of other bird-watchers learnt our trade. The result of years of work by its original author, the late Austin Roberts, it was first published in 1940. Since that time Roberts, as it is affectionately known, has been revised several times by a succession of editors, most recently by Prof. Gordon Lindsay Maclean. Opinions about the status of this book differ, I know, but I regard Roberts as a handbook, not a fieldguide. As such it gives a much greater depth of detail about each bird than is possible in a fieldguide and, for those of us who seek to know a little more about our birds and their lives, Roberts is the answer. It not only illustrates all southern Africa's species but gives descriptions of eggs, nests, breeding seasons, etc. as well. I advise all serious bird-watchers to have a copy of Roberts on their bookshelves as a back-up to their Newman's.

Spend a little time paging through bird books; study the pictures and read the text. The more information you digest about birds, their appearance, voice and habits, the more easily you'll get to grips with unfamiliar species when you see them.

Binoculars and telescopes

Before you can put your fieldguide to use you need to be able to see the bird clearly, and that calls for binoculars. No matter how keen one's sight, distant or tiny birds cannot be properly examined without an optical aid, and binoculars are the obvious

Don't let birding become a pain in the neck ...
binoculars should be light and comfortable

choice. Telescopes are also a good investment but we'll talk about them later.

Today there are so many binoculars available, of varying sizes and prices, that the buyer may be justifiably nonplussed. However there are a few golden rules to bear in mind. First, pay as much as you can afford; it will prove a worthwhile investment. Don't try to economise with a cheap pair of binoculars since cheap lenses may impair the vision. They are also likely to fall out of alignment before long since the internal prisms are merely glued into place. Binoculars should not be so heavy that you cannot hold them steady. They should also feel light and comfortable when hanging around your neck, or you may discover that a few hours of birding can literally be a pain in the neck! If you wear spectacles get binoculars that have roll-back rubber eyepieces.

For bird-watching I recommend roof-prism binoculars as opposed to the more conventional barrel-type binoculars since they are more compact and easier to hold (see illustrations). For instance roof-prism binoculars with a magnifying power of 10 times will be considerably smaller than barrel-type binoculars of the same power, but they are usually more expensive.

8 x 40 barrel-type binoculars

The best binoculars for bird-watching are within the range of 7,5 x 30, 8 x 35 and 10 x 40. The first number is always the magnification, so that 8 x binoculars will enlarge the bird eight times. The second number is the millimetre diameter of the large front lenses. Thus in 8 x 35 binoculars the front lenses each have a diameter of 35 mm. The larger the diameter of the front lenses the *wider the field of view and the brighter the image seen.* Image brightness is particularly important when viewing birds in poor light, and a wide field of view facilitates locating the bird, especially in flight, through the binoculars. I personally prefer 10 x 40 roof-prism binoculars because they are moderately light, powerful, and provide a bright image.

Don't hurry your binoculars purchase. Examine and handle many before you finally decide. If a pair of binoculars feel comfortable in your hand, test them by going to the shop door and focusing on some object across the road or further down the shopping mall. (Be sure that the optical adjustment is on neutral

10 x 42 roof-prism binoculars

or is adjusted to your eyes; the salesperson will show you how to do this.) The image must be sharp and clear without any colour aberration. Should the image be surrounded by a colour outline the lenses will be inferior and possibly harmful to your eyes.

Compact roof-prism binoculars suitable for the handbag or shirt pocket are also popular, and are particularly useful when travelling. Compact binoculars are very small and usually come in 8 x 20, 10 x 22 or thereabouts. However, since the front lenses are small their light gathering capability is low and the field of view very narrow, but as a second pair for travel or emergencies they are certainly handy.

Rubber-coated binoculars may be splash-proof or even fully waterproof according to the make, and are certainly worth considering if you contemplate bird-watching in wet conditions. The rubber coating is also useful in protecting the binoculars from knocks and bumps.

While I do not recommend that you buy a telescope initially there will probably come a time you feel the need, and this is

Compact 8 x 24 roof-prism binoculars

especially true when looking at distant shorebirds. Telescopes also require a steady tripod, so one is faced with extra paraphernalia to carry. If you decide to buy a telescope for bird-watching the rules are similar to those for binoculars: seek something that gives a bright image and is not too bulky. One can get bird-watching scopes with magnifications ranging from 16 x to 60 x, and some have zoom lenses. I use a small, compact scope with a magnification of 32 x and find it ideal. Its light-gathering qualities are superb and the image cannot be matched for clarity. A point to remember is that the greater the magnification the less clear the image and, with Africa's great heat, a powerful lens will pick up so much heat haze that the object of one's scrutiny is often distorted.

One last point about telescopes. They come with straight-through or angled eyepieces, and the choice is purely a personal one. The straight-through eyepiece often allows one to pick up the bird more speedily but it may also involve much stooping and neck-craning unless the tripod is at the correct height. When the bird is close by and high in a tree the angled eyepiece will certainly be easier on the neck.

Notebook and pencil

So much for the expenses. The next and final piece of equipment you should arm yourself with is a small notebook and pencil or ballpoint pen. Cultivate the habit of making notes of the birds you have seen, and particularly when you are not sure what you have seen. A simple sketch, no matter how crude, with field notes about beak, legs, colours, habitat, etc. will prove essential when you page through your fieldguide over a sun-downer that evening trying to identify 'the one that got away' or 'the bird that isn't in Newman's book'.

Learn from friends

I cannot over-emphasise the advantage of going into the field with helpful, experienced birders; it's the quickest way to learn the features of the various bird species. Bird clubs, with their weekend and day outings, provide this essential service so, if there's a club near you, why not tag along? You'll also find that the local bird club will give periodic lectures about birds by their more experienced members, usually accompanied by slides or films, and in addition provide a quarterly bird maga-zine and a newsletter about forthcoming activities.

WHERE TO LOOK FOR BIRDS

In Africa birds are everywhere; even the Namib desert has birds that can be found nowhere else while the Karoo is a bird par-adise if you know what you're looking for. On the other hand there certainly are many places and habitats that have a richer avifauna than others, and one is best advised to become familiar with these prime habitats.

Bushveld

This is a term sometimes applied loosely to any indigenous wooded region whether the vegetation be bushes, trees or a mixture of both, but whatever its make-up it is likely to be a very productive bird habitat. Bushveld covers vast areas of the land both within nature reserves and without, and so far as birds are concerned it falls into the two broad categories of thornveld and broadleaved woodland; sometimes a mixture of both. Thornveld, or a habitat comprising mostly thorn bushes, is highly attractive to many birds, not only those that feed in the thorny canopies but also the ground-feeders. I cannot explain this phenomenon and have yet to meet anyone who can, but it is a fact. When birding in bushveld I head for patches of thorn-veld for preference and can be sure to find a rich selection of insectivorous, frugivorous and granivorous bird species. Within bushveld watch the ground for francolins, guineafowl, sandgrouse, larks and waxbills. Check the lower stratum of the bushes for tchagra shrikes, boubous and prinias, the canopy for bush shrikes, titbabblers, eremomelas and other warblers. At higher levels watch out for flycatchers, drongoes, starlings, weavers, barbets and sunbirds while some of the taller trees may harbour sunbirds, woodpeckers and birds of prey.

A bird party is made up of many different species of birds, all feeding in harmony and in close proximity.

Broadleafed woodland

African broadleafed woodland, in which the grassy understory is fairly open and in which the trees are so spaced that their canopies do not touch, supports a number of canopy-feeding birds that may not be found in thornveld. These include certain flycatchers, shrikes and woodpeckers. The main difference between this and other habitats is that bird inhabitants of woodland normally occur in what are called 'bird parties'. Within woodland one can walk for 10 to 15 minutes without seeing many birds at all then, suddenly, one comes across a bird party and is hard put to note them all. A bird party is made up of many different species of birds, all feeding in harmony and in close proximity. It may contain for example drongoes, flycatchers, shrikes, woodpeckers, orioles, warblers and sunbirds, depending on its location. There may be some protective advantage to mixed feeding in that the birds have a better chance collectively of spotting the approach of an aerial predator such as a sparrowhawk, but this has not been conclusively proved. Whatever the reason it is worth remembering that some birds are likely to be found only in bird parties within woodland, and this is particularly true of the Miombo woodlands of Zimbabwe, Zambia and Malawi where the Brachystegia tree is dominant.

Wetlands

This is another name applied broadly to a wide variety of waterways and other moist situations. Most wetlands are very productive for the bird-watcher: they harbour an almost endless variety of ducks, geese, moorhens, coots, grebes, herons, spoonbills, flamingoes, gulls, terns, small waders and the many water-associated reed-dwelling birds. Inland there are numerous dams and natural pans where one can spend many fulfilling hours of bird-watching, and some of the better municipal and provincial bird sanctuaries have waters that can be observed from hides specially built for the purpose.

At the coast, in addition to the shoreline, one should visit river estuaries and coastal lagoons which are usually rich in waterbirds while the dune forests and coastal bush may be good for coucals, louries, barbets, sunbirds, waxbills and some of the not-so-easy-to-see doves.

Still on the subject of wetlands municipal sewage disposal plants are a must and are favourite venues for bird clubs. In most cases the manager in charge will permit entry to *bona fide* bird-watchers and, although the atmosphere may be a little strong sometimes, the larger settlement pans attract numerous waterbirds.

Evergreen forests

Not to be confused with the sterile plantations of exotic trees such as pines and eucalypts that are planted for timber. Evergreen forests are very old and include a great variety of indigenous trees. Evergreen forests are found in regions that receive good annual rains and can be separated into lowland forests and high altitude forests. Our lowland forests occur along the eastern seaboard while the high altitude forests are found in the mistbelt, especially along the Drakensberg escarpment that runs northwards to the northern Transvaal. Good examples of lowland forest may be found in the Knysna and Port Elizabeth regions and in Zululand, while the most extensive high altitude forest is the Woodbush Forest Reserve at Magoebaskloof between Pietersburg and Tzaneen in the northern Transvaal.

Evergreen forests harbour many special birds unlikely to be found elsewhere, but be warned that finding them calls for a lot of patience and perseverance. The forests themselves are dense and are frequently in hilly regions so that one is mostly standing on inclines of 45 degrees or more or clutching at the nearest tree while attempting to train one's binoculars on a bird in the canopy 30 metres above. Forest birding becomes very hard on the neck once one has left the beaten track, and sometimes even on the beaten track! The best plan by far is to follow the tracks and trails and especially to sit quietly for 20 minutes or so. It's surprising how active birds become when they believe that human intruders have passed. The best times for forest birding are spring and early summer when most birds are actively breeding and calling. At these times the calls of the Narina Trogon, Knysna Lourie and many others can be heard through much of the day while, at night, the Wood Owl can be heard. At other times first and last light are best. Then one can hear the Orange Thrush, Brown and Chorister Robins in full voice.

Perhaps the most spectacular of the forest birds is the Crowned Eagle, but it is more likely to be seen flying than perched. Each morning the Crowned Eagles indulge in a lengthy territorial display flight, either one bird or two, diving and zooming upwards while calling a far-carrying 'keweee, keweee, keweee....'. Another spectacle to watch for is the flight of the Knysna Lourie with its bright scarlet wing feathers or the passing of a flock of Cape Parrots heralding their arrival with shrill screeches. In fact the presence of many forest birds is best detected by their calls. In this way one can locate the Squaretailed Drongo, Olive and Blackfronted Bush Shrikes, Yellowstreaked Bulbul, Yellowthroated Warbler and the Natal, Chorister, Brown and Starred Robins which include some of our finest songsters. Many forest birds, the robins in particular as well as Terrestrial Bulbuls, Cinnamon and Tambourine Doves feed on the ground; another good reason for sitting quietly (if the ants don't get you!).

Riverine bush or forest

Many rivers have well-wooded banks and some have such well-developed trees as to qualify as forests. This riverine growth, with its fruiting and seeding trees, is invariably good for birds of all kinds, including louries, flycatchers, cuckooshrikes, birds of prey and, during summer, migrant cuckoos and kingfishers.

Grasslands

Don't ignore the grasslands; they harbour many interesting birds from larks to korhaans, warblers to cranes and are particularly alive with activity during the early summer months when many of the widows and bishops adopt their colourful breeding plumages, and all are making their presence known by call. During the dry season this activity slows down somewhat; many of the more colourful species revert to their dull, non-breeding colours and stop calling. Perhaps as a beginner one should not start in grasslands since there are so many little brown birds that defy recognition. Rather keep this habitat up your sleeve until you are feeling a little more confident; you'll then find it very rewarding.

Gardens

As I mentioned at the start one's own garden, if well bushed and treed, is a good place in which to become familiar with local birds, and the best way to attract them is with food and water. Obviously the avian content of your garden will depend on where you live, but whatever the species there are few that can resist a good meal or bath. My book *Newman's Garden Birds* provides most of the answers to garden birding, but I'll repeat some tips here: hang a swinging bird table from a branch or mount the table on a vertical pole and keep it well stocked with goodies. The table itself can be an old wooden tray or piece of wood or chipboard. Bird seeds (expensive) or crushed maize (cheaper) plus dampened stale bread will attract sparrows, doves and weavers. The seed or crushed maize can be supplied in a commercial bird-feeder or merely scattered on the table or even the ground if there are no cats. Should you wish to attract the more colourful fruit-eaters such as bulbuls, barbets and louries then give them old apples, pears and pawpaws. Damaged or overripe fruit can usually be obtained from the local greengrocer for a few cents (the better ones give it free), otherwise put out your apple and pear cores and pawpaw skins for the birds. I have found these fruits to be the most favoured but others have found that they will take tomatoes, guavas and even peas.

To attract the insect-eaters such as robins, flycatchers and wagtails there is nothing quite as good as butcher's bonemeal: the residue from meat and bones cut on the circular saw. Ask your butcher for some; the birds go crazy for it. I have also found that nearly all birds will eat maize meal (mealie pap) and Epol dog food mixed into a paste with water.

Finally water. Birds love to bathe, and many, such as doves and pigeons, need to drink. Either a garden pond or raised bird bath is recommended. If you have a pond and keep it stocked with goldfish you are likely to be visited by kingfishers and herons, but please don't get angry when you see a fish being swallowed. Isn't that why you put them there?

WHEN TO LOOK FOR BIRDS

The majority of birds are with us all the time, but a few are season-al migrants. Birds generally are most active during the mornings from dawn until about 10h00, and in the evenings from about 16h30 till last light. During the middle of the day they tend to rest or at least be less active, even when feeding young and during hot weather. The exceptions are the high-flying eagles and vultures, but even these are most active during the first half of the day. Nocturnal birds, owls, nightjars and dikkops are most active between dusk and midnight, longer when the moon is bright. Nightjars do most of their feeding in the first hour or two of dark-ness and can often be seen flying around at dusk.

Migratory birds fall into two groups, local and long distance migrants, and both move seasonally, usually departing in late sum-mer and returning in spring. We call those that migrate within Africa the intra-Africa migrants and those that come from the northern hemisphere (which is called the Palaearctic Region) the Palaearctic migrants. Many of these migrants come to us as non-breeding visitors, a few come here to breed. These migrants include birds of prey, shorebirds, small warblers, swallows and many oth-ers. When reading about a bird in your fieldguide check whether it is a resident species or a migrant. If the latter you'll know that it's unlikely to be here between May and August.

HOW TO LOOK AT BIRDS

You need to look at a strange bird in such a way that you will recall its salient features once it has flown. Birds do have the infuriating habit of disappearing just as you get the binoculars focused on them. The following tips should prove useful.

It's a good idea to have a system for looking at unfamiliar birds, and the one that I have devised can, with a little practice, be committed to memory so that you will run through the pro-cedure almost subconsciously. There are six stages:

(1) Decide upon its approximate size.
(2) Check its beak.
(3) Check its legs.
(4) Note any bold markings or colours.
(5) Note the habitat it is in.
(6) Note what it is doing.

I will explain . . .

1. What size is the bird?
The size of the bird is very important. It doesn't help later to say it was quite large or quite small. Decide upon the approximate size of the bird by comparing it with three well-known birds. Is the bird larger or smaller than a sparrow? If it is larger, then is it larger or smaller than a city pigeon? If larger is it larger or smaller than a guineafowl? Try to establish this in your mind while examining the bird.

2. Beak shape and colour
Beaks or bills are an important aid to identifying a bird. The beak may be long and slender as in some wading birds; it may be curved downward like that of a bee-eater or sunbird, or upwards as in the Avocet; it may be short and stout as seen in the seed-eating sparrows, weavers and canaries or it can be hooked as in a bird of prey or parrot. Some birds have coloured beaks. These points need to be memorised.

3. Leg length and colour
Legs are also very important clues that help identify a bird. Are its legs 'normal' length in proportion to its body size, as seen for example in a sparrow or thrush? They may be long, even very long as seen in many waterbirds, or very short as seen in bee-eaters and swallows. If the legs are long what colour are they?

4. Plumage colours and markings
The colours or plumage markings that first strike you should be memorised. Note whether the bird has colour on its head, breast, tail or wings, and if it has any bold markings such as a white wing-bar or black band across its breast. These could provide vital clues.

5. What is the habitat?
It is important to note the habitat in which you see the bird, because this also gives an important lead to its identity since certain look-alikes are found in totally different habitats.

6. What is the bird doing?
The bird's behaviour is another important clue to its identity. If the bird is in a tree then what is it doing in that tree? It could be

feeding in the outer leaves of the canopy (flycatcher) or sitting within the canopy (warbler). It could be perched on top of the tree (shrike or drongo) or on one side of the tree (roller or kingfisher). The bird could be pecking at the tree trunk or branches (woodpecker or barbet). It might be swimming, wading, flying or merely walking.

The six foregoing points, whether remembered or written in your notebook, will help you to decide on the bird's identity (ID) when reading the fieldguide descriptions of those you think it could have been. As I have said above this procedure becomes second nature with a little practice.

THE MAGIC ID FORMULA

1 Decide upon its approximate size

2 Check its beak

3 Check its legs

4 Note any bold markings or colours

5 Note the habitat it is in

6 Note what it is doing

JIZZ

It is also a good thing to learn the 'jizz' of the various bird families. This strange word refers to the bird's general shape and size, or the impression it makes on you when you first see it. Each bird family has its own peculiar jizz. When we look, for example, at the common Cattle Egret we know that it belongs to the heron family, not only because it has long legs and a longish neck (many other bird families have these things) but because of the specific posture of this group of birds: their jizz. Likewise we all know what a wagtail looks like, and how it walks. If you were to see a similar bird with bright blue or pink colouring you would recognise it as a wagtail of sorts because of its strutting manner and bobbing tail: its jizz.

There are often many species of birds within a family. In southern Africa we have 13 robins and 18 related chats and their allies, all of which have a similar jizz. There are 13 different starlings and they too have a distinctive family jizz, as do the sunbirds, bee-eaters, woodpeckers, etc. etc. I cannot stress too strongly the importance of becoming familiar with the jizz of the different bird families as soon as possible, and it can be

THE TYPICAL JIZZ OF THE LAZY CISTICOLA .

The typical jizz of a robin, chat, thrush and starling

The typical jizz of a sunbird, bee-eater and woodpecker

achieved by studying the illustrations in your Newman's field-guide. Sit and look carefully at the robins, chats and their allies the rockjumpers and wheatears. They are all quite closely related and share not only similar body shapes and sizes but also postures, such as the tail-up stance and jerky, alert movements.

Study the ducks and note how most of them stand with their bodies in the horizontal position. At your local dam, or even at the zoo, you can see how ducks waddle when they walk; this is because their legs are widely spaced and placed in the middle of their bodies. No other waterbirds walk in such a fashion. These things plus the duck's spatulate bill all add up to its familiar jizz. In contrast the whistling ducks, represented by the Whitefaced and Fulvous Ducks (page 87 in my fieldguide), being more closely related to geese, have an erect stance and

The jizz of dabbling and whistling ducks

walk without waddling. This is because their legs are less widely spaced and are placed further back on their bodies.

Get to know the jizz of the shrikes (pages 371-81). Notice their rather bulky bodies, their heavy-headed appearance and their strong, hooked beaks. The shrikes can also be divided into four distinct groups. All those on page 371 of the fieldguide plus the Fiscal Shrike on page 373 and Sousa's Shrike on page 375 habitually perch in an exposed position, maybe on a tree or a telephone wire, from where they seize insects on the ground. The boubous and bush shrikes tend to seek their food within the canopy of trees and bushes. Tchagra shrikes mostly forage on

The jizz of various shrikes

the ground or in the lower strata while the helmetshrikes flutter in groups from tree to tree. In these cases the birds' identities can be established by a combination of plumage colouring, jizz and habits.

WHY FISCAL SHRIKE?

Many years ago taxes in the Cape Colony were collected by the Fiscal Tax Collector whose uniform was black and white. The tax collector was feared because he had the authority to whip defaulters. It seems that the black and white plumage of the shrike, equally feared by other small birds for its predatory habits, earned it the name of Fiscal Shrike. Since the Fiscal Flycatcher has a similar plumage it is obliged to share the same epithet.

HOW TO USE YOUR FIELDGUIDE

Beginners are often dismayed by the enormous array of birds shown in the fieldguide: nearly 900 species for southern Africa alone. Even more baffling is the question of finding the page showing the bird you want.

The first step is to become familiar with the major groupings and families of birds. The reason is that when you see an unfamiliar bird, you need to decide what group or family it belongs to so that you know where in the fieldguide to start looking for it. Trying to page through the whole fieldguide to find the bird (which by now will have flown away!) will soon prove futile.

Locating each bird group has been made much easier in the most recent editions of my fieldguide: they have an easy-to-use index, large page numbers and colour-coding. However, for those using an older edition I recommend that you divide it into sections yourself. This can be done either as a temporary measure by inserting slips of paper between the pages of the sections or by tabbing the pages. Ready-gummed page tabs can be bought at stationers, and these can be marked with the name of the bird group in that section.

The first section in the book will be the ocean birds, pages 28-60. Those birders living inland with little contact with the sea may seldom need to refer to this first section and may even want to put an elastic band around it until that holiday at Margate. The next section should be called inland waterbirds, and it will also start at page 60 because the last three birds on that page frequent inland waters, not the sea; inland waterbirds will end on page 85. The next section will be ducks and wading birds (the wading birds are all those that make a living walking in the water or on the shoreline), pages 86-127; then come the larger terrestrial birds (those often long-legged birds that inhabit dry land), pages 128-51; followed by birds of prey, pages 152-93; sandgrouse, doves, parrots, louries, cuckoos and coucals, pages 194-215; the nocturnal owls and nightjars, pages 216-28; the aerial-feeding swallows and swifts, pages 228-47; mousebirds and hole-nesters (birds that nest in holes in trees or banks, namely bee-eaters, kingfishers, rollers, hoopoes, hornbills, barbets, woodpeckers and honeyguides), pages 244-73; the next lot, slender-billed insect-eating birds, form a large group and so I break them into two sections, part 1 larks to robins, pages 276-331, and part 2 warblers to starlings and oxpeckers, pages 332-

89; then come the nectar-feeders (the sugarbirds, sunbirds and white-eyes), pages 388-403; and finally the stout-billed seedeaters, pages 404-43.

THE PARTS OF A BIRD

CROWN
SUPERCILIARY
EYE STRIPE
LATERAL CROWN STRIPE
CREST
LORES
FOREHEAD
CERE
FRONT
MALAR STRIPE
CULMEN
UPPER MANDIBLE
EAR COVERTS
GULAR STRIPE
NAIL
MOUSTACIAL STRIPE
LOWER MANDIBLE
CHIN
GAPE
ORBITAL RING
THROAT
NAPE
BREAST
MANTLE
WATTLES
HIND NECK
SCAPULARS
LESSER COVERTS
CARPAL JOINT
MEDIAN WING COVERTS
GREATER WING COVERTS
BELLY
SECONDARIES
LESSER COVERTS
BACK
THIGH
TERTIALS
ALULA
TERTIALS
RUMP
TIBIA
GREATER COVERTS
UPPER TAIL COVERTS
TIBIO-TARSAL JOINT
SECONDARIES
VENT
TARSUS
UNDER TAIL COVERTS
HIND TOE
PRIMARIES

UPPER WING PLAN

GREATER WING COVERTS
MEDIAN COVERTS
ALULA
MARGINAL COVERTS
MEDIAN PRIMARY COVERTS
GREATER PRIMARY COVERTS
SCAPULARS
TERTIALS
SPECULUM (DUCKS ONLY)
SECONDARIES
PRIMARIES

IDENTITY UNMASKED
finding the bird in your fieldguide

When you've seen an unfamiliar bird that you want to identify, the first step is to decide which family or group you think it belongs to. Turn to page ix, where the various groups are colour-coded, find that colour section in the fieldguide and look at the illustrations. Is there one that resembles the bird you've seen? If yes, check the distribution map and, if it shows that the bird could occur in your region, read the description. If all things fit, you've identified your bird. Should either the description, distribution or habitat be wrong for your bird, you need to look again at the pictures and also at other possible bird groups. Continue along these lines until you've identified your bird.

If it should happen that the description and the distribution map fit but the colours of the bird don't look exactly like those of the bird you've seen, don't panic! There are often slight differences in birds' colouring — even major differences in the case of young raptors or when birds are changing from their summer to winter plumages or vice versa. A useful guide to remember is that in-between colours will still occur in the same places on the bird as its full adult or breeding pattern. For example a bird that has a black head and a white breast in adult plumage may be seen as an immature with a brownish or mottled head, but in the same pattern as that of the adult. Examine the illustration in the fieldguide on page 169 of a young Fish Eagle, the one marked Ja; note that it has not yet assumed the adult white head and breast and yet the colour pattern follows that of the adult.

Although these bird groupings may appear to be arbitrary ones they nevertheless tend to incorporate birds of similar habits or food preferences. When studied carefully, and with use, the logic of these divisions will become apparent, and familiarity with them will prove helpful in locating the bird you are seeking in the fieldguide.

216   OWLS

Owls. Families TYTONIDAE and STRIGIDAE. Nocturnal, erect-standing birds of prey, characterised by large, rounded heads, large forward-facing eyes set in a flattened face and feathered legs (except for Pel's Fishing Owl). Some have feather adornments on their heads which resemble ears. Immatures are usually darker, fluffier than adults.

1 MARSH OWL *Asio capensis.* Common to uncommon resident. Medium-sized, dark brown owl with small 'ear' tufts; shows russet wings in flight. Sometimes calls 'kraak' in flight. Singly or in pairs in long grass in marshy ground, vleis and near dams. Often active early mornings and late afternoons, flying low or perched on a fence pole. When flushed from the grass during daytime flies in circles over the in[...]der before resettling. 36 cm. 396

2 WOOD OWL *Strix woodfordii.* Fairly common, localised resident. Told by lack of 'ears', large pale, spectacle-like eye-orbits and barred underparts. Immatures with [...]ter eye-orbits and [...]ker colouring. Males call a rapid 'HU-hu, hu[...]U-hu-hu, hu-hu', fe[...]les reply with a higher-pitched 'hoo'. Pairs [...] family groups in t[...]sts, well-developed riverine forests and exotic plantations. Duri[...] the day roosts in large trees close to the tru[...]. 30-6 cm. 394

3 BARN [...] WL *Tyto alba.* Common resident. A pale, slim[...]built owl with h[...]t-shaped facial disc and whitish underparts, [...]ld from the ne[...] species by paler upperparts. The call is an eerie, wavering scre[...]h. Singly or in pairs in a variety of habitats, roosting and [...]eding in large trees, caves, buildings and Hamerkop nests [...]age 81); common in suburbia. 30-3 cm. 392

4 GRASS OWL *Tyto [...]apensis.* Uncommon resident. Closely similar to the previous species but distinguished by darker upperparts and different [...]abitat. Hisses when disturbed; also makes a husky screech rese[...]bling the call of the Barn Owl. Singly or in pairs in moist grassland. When disturbed during the day flies directly away and resettles; c[...] Marsh Owl (1). 34-7 cm. 383

217

1

2

3

4

PASSERINE BIRDS

This is a term that terrifies some people, but it need not. Passerine is a name given to birds that are otherwise known as songbirds or perching birds. These are simply all the little birds that have melodious voices or the typical perching foot, or both. Let's look at the perching foot first. It's a foot that is able to grip slender perches such as small twigs, grass stems and wires; it has three toes facing forward and one facing backwards, and all four toes are joined at the same level; *this is important*.

A songbird's foot is able to encircle its perch. Furthermore, when the bird settles down on its perch to sleep, relaxing the upper leg so that its body sinks downward, tendons within its leg become taught, pulling the toes closed so that the foot locks onto the perch. It will only unlock when the bird wakes and stands again to relax the tendons. Now you know why small birds don't get blown off their perches at night. In normal perching activities on a horizontal perch a songbird doesn't need to grip its perch tightly; in most instances its grip is quite relaxed.

When a passerine or songbird relaxes on a perch it bends its leg which causes the main flexor tendon to pull the toes into a firm grip (A).

In order to relax its grip the bird must extend its legs by standing (B)

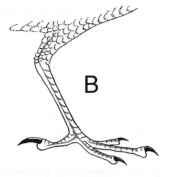

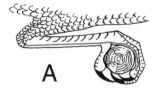

The term 'songbird' itself doesn't necessarily indicate that birds of this group all sing well, although most do have a song of sorts. The largest perching birds or songbirds are the crow family, and one would hardly describe their harsh squawks as songs. The sparrows and weavers for instance are also part of the songbird group although they only twitter and swizzle. Others have calls as well as songs.

All those birds that are not passerines (songbirds) are simply called non-passerines; they do not sing and they lack a true perching foot. They include all the seabirds, herons, ducks, storks, pheasants, raptors, pigeons, cuckoos, coucals, louries, owls, nightjars, swifts, woodpeckers, barbets, rollers, hornbills and hoopoes; in fact all the birds in your fieldguide up to and including the Spotted Creeper on page 275. The only exception (in Newman's fieldguide) are the swallows on pages 228-38, which are true passerines. I put them next to the swifts (which are non-passerines) simply to facilitate comparison.

A look at the non-passerines between pages 28 and 275 will show birds with bills of various lengths and shapes, legs long and short and specialised feet in which the toes do not always number four and are not always joined at the same level; webbed feet, three-toed feet and zygodactylous feet in which two toes may point forward and two backwards. Non-passerines do not sing; they may grunt, squawk, squeak, quack, trumpet or hoot but they have no utterances remotely resembling a song. There is certainly no such thing as a swan-song!

Now that you know that page 275 is the divider between the non-passerines and the passerines have a closer look, first, at the non-passerines (non-songbirds if you prefer) and just see what an odd assortment they are. An interesting lot but none that could be described as perching birds or songbirds. This is not to say that they cannot perch. Even storks and ducks can perch in trees, but their feet are not adapted to *grasping* a perch in the way that a true passerine is able to do. Many of the larger birds merely *stand* on a tree, and may raise their wings in order to maintain balance in a wind. Storks and large herons do this. Other non-passerines have feet designed for clinging, and these include the woodpeckers, which have the zygodactylous feet already described, and the swifts which cling to vertical surfaces such as rocks. Raptors have powerful feet armed with sharp talons for holding and crushing their prey while many waterbirds have webbed or semi-webbed feet as aids to swimming.

Various foot types

The legs of non-passerines also show great variation, in length especially. Those that make their living walking in water or in long grass tend to have long legs, and these include the herons, storks, cranes and bustards, while some have long legs to facilitate running, such as the coursers and the Ostrich. Many have short legs, for example the swifts and nightjars, because they feed in the air and walk very little.

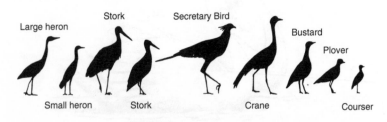

Some long-legged non-passerines

| Starling | Bulbul | Chat | Fiscal Shrike |

Typical passerines

When you have studied the non-passerine birds turn to the passerines with their perching feet. You will see that they all have legs proportionate to their body size; what might be termed 'normal' length legs. The one exception is the swallow family which, like the totally unrelated swifts, have little need to walk.

SCIENTIFIC NAMES

Why do birds (and other living things) have scientific names in addition to their vernacular names?

The scientific system of naming living things was started by the Swedish naturalist Linnaeus in the eighteenth century. Under this simple system all living organisms are given two names, the first name is for the genus (the generic name) and the second is for the species (the specific name). A genus is a group of closely related species; a species is all members of a genus that, under normal circumstances, will interbreed. Since this system is internationally recognised there can be no confusion as to which organism is being referred to between scientists anywhere in the world. In contrast vernacular names, in whatever language, are subject to changes according to local preference. One bird may have several popular names and this can lead to great confusion.

DID YOU KNOW?

The beak colour of many bird species acts as a stimulant to the nestlings, causing them to open their beaks on seeing that particular colour. The Cattle Egret, for instance, in common with many other herons, assumes brighter bill colours when it's breeding. In the case of the egret the normally yellow bill becomes temporarily deep orange with a reddish base. On seeing this the nestlings immediately start pecking at the parent's bill which, in turn, encourages the parent to regurgitate the partially digested food it has brought for its offspring. Some years ago I cut out of cardboard a number of imitation Cattle Egret 'bills' and painted all except one in various colours such as plain yellow, green and blue. On presenting these strangely coloured bills to Cattle Egret nestlings they showed no interest whatever, but when presented with a 'bill' of the correct colours they pecked at it vigorously.

In other species colour stimulation works both ways, not only do the nestlings respond to beak, throat or head colours of their parents but the parents themselves react to the colours, or colour patterns, inside their nestlings' mouths. A good example of this is seen in the Orangethroated Longclaw (page 290 in the fieldguide). Both sexes have bright orange throats, and this colour is repeated exactly in the interior of its nestlings' mouths; both young and parents respond to the colour orange. On seeing the parent arrive at the nest the chicks respond not to the food in the parent's beak but to the colour orange, which causes them to open their mouths wide; the parent in turn responds to the bright orange of its chick's mouth and thrusts food into it.

Other well known instances of this nature are seen in the mouth interiors of nestling waxbills and their allies, some of which have quite complicated patterns of coloured spots.

BILLS OR BEAKS

I have already touched on the importance of beaks under the section above entitled 'How to look at birds', but it may not be realised that the shape of a bird's beak is often a guide to its diet — which, in turn, is a clue to its identity. Incidentally, beaks and bills are synonymous; I prefer to call the small ones beaks and the large ones bills but there is no written law. As a piece of useless information beaks and bills are, technically, the bird's rostrum, but I wouldn't lose any sleep over it.

A bird's beak is its principal tool, and is used for feeding, digging, probing, carrying, plumage-preening, nest-building and fighting. In some storks bill-clapping is used as a greeting between mated pairs at the nest while in others, such as the Saddlebilled Stork, the bill colours may play a part in courtship.

| Hoopoe | Sunbird | Flycatcher | Shrike | Waxbill |

Beaks vary according to diet

If we look at the sparrows, weavers, widowbirds, whydahs, waxbills and canaries (pages 404-42) we will see short, stout, conical beaks suited to the crushing of hard seeds and grain, the principal diet of this group. In contrast the slender, decurved beaks of the sunbirds (pages 390-401) and the sugarbirds (page 389) are the specialised tools of flower-probing nectar-eaters. Some of the most nectar-rich flowers are the tubular kind, as seen in aloes. When a sunbird is unable to reach the nectar with its long beak and tongue it probes through the side of the blossom instead. Sunbirds are small with a body size less than that of a sparrow in many cases, their movements rapid and erratic as they flit from flower to flower. The sugarbirds, being larger than sunbirds, have a more direct flight and tend to favour protea flowers. Another group of birds with longish, decurved beaks are the bee-eaters (pages 244-7), but there should be no confusion between these and the sunbirds, although both display brilliant colours. Bee-eaters are larger than sparrows, smaller bodied than pigeons but, with their extended tail-shafts, some may be longer. Bee-eaters are mostly seen in flocks, the

WHY KINGFISHER?

Not all kingfishers feed on fish; many eat insects instead. Of southern Africa's ten kingfishers half are insectivorous. They are the Woodland, Greyhooded, Brownhooded, Striped and Pygmy Kingfishers. However, don't be surprised if you should one day see one of these kingfishers plunging into water. I have seen the Woodland, Brownhooded, Greyhooded and Pygmy Kingfishers do this occasionally; they are either bathing, catching insects on the surface or have broken away from tradition temporarily by succumbing to the temptation of a small fish near the surface.

exception being the Little Bee-eater which occurs in pairs or small family groups. They catch flying insects in the air, and usually return to a perch where they immobilise the prey before eating it. This is done by holding the bee (or other insect) in the tip of the beak while beating it against the perch. They breed in tunnels excavated in earth banks.

Kingfishers, hoopoes, woodhoopoes and hornbills all have longish bills. In the case of the kingfishers (pages 248-52) their bills are used for catching and holding fish which they then, after the fashion of the bee-eaters, beat into immobility. However, some kingfishers don't catch fish: they feed on insects and small reptiles caught away from water, but still they have the long bill. Hoopoes and the related woodhoopoes (page 257) use their decurved bills for probing, in the case of the Hoopoe for probing in the soil and, in the woodhoopoes, for probing beneath the bark of trees. Hornbills, on the other hand (pages 258-63), could consume their diet of insects and fruit quite easily without such huge bills but, because their bills are light of weight and mostly hollow, they serve as amplifiers to give resonance to the birds' calls.

Moderately long, chisel-like bills are found in the woodpeckers (pages 266-70) and are necessary tools for excavating nest holes in trees and, coupled with their long tongues, for probing beneath bark and into crevices in search of insects and their larvae.

Many water-associated birds have long, slender beaks. They probe into the soil or mud in search of insects, crustaceans and molluscs. Such birds often have long legs too and may be seen wading on the shorelines of coastal and inland waters, or in marshy regions and moist grasslands. They are the ibises, snipes and other shorebirds that are illustrated and described on pages 84 and 104-26. Note that the ibises' bills are decurved. In contrast the Avocet (page 127) has a long, slender bill that is turned upwards, or recurved.

Long bills are also found in the storks (pages 76-81) and larger herons (pages 72-5). The storks' bills are robust and are used for catching and holding fish, frogs and other small animals, while those of the herons are for stabbing or thrusting at fish, an action that is aided by their long necks. Many of the smaller herons have only moderately long bills and shorter necks, and when these birds thrust at a fish they throw their entire bodies forward. Two herons, the Blackheaded (page 74) and the Cattle Egret (page 72) seldom eat fish but prefer insects, reptiles and small mammals caught away from water.

The well-hooked bills of the birds of prey are obviously an adaptation to flesh-tearing, and this applies equally to the huge vultures (pages 152-7), the smallest kestrels (page 193) and the owls (pages 216-22). But the parrots (pages 202-5) put their hooked bills to a different use, that of splitting and cracking the hard outer shells of seedpods to extract the kernels. Since many shrikes (pages 370-81) also kill small birds, reptiles and rodents, and will steal birds' eggs and nestlings given the chance, they too have hooked beaks for flesh-tearing.

The insectivorous birds form a very large group, while many seed-eaters and nectar-feeders also eat insects. However, those birds that are predominantly insectivorous will be seen to have fairly short, slender beaks. Good examples of these are the chats, robins, warblers and flycatchers illustrated between pages 316 and 369 of the fieldguide. Many of the aerial-feeding insect-eaters, the nightjars, swallows and swifts (pages 224-43), have quite short beaks but wide gapes. They feed by flying with their mouths open, so the wide gape provides the equivalent of an enlarged catching-net. This group of birds also shares another feature: very short legs, since they do little walking.

BIRD SONGS

The sounds made by birds fall into two categories: songs and calls. Songs are usually of a territorial nature and are uttered mostly by the male to keep others of its species away from its selected territory; a sort of warning advertisement. Calls, on the other hand, are mostly used as contacts between pairs or groups, some soft, others louder. Why the Hadedas need to belt out their calls in such a deafening manner is not properly understood, but it can in no way be rated as a song!

Bird songs and calls are a valuable aid to knowing a species, even when one cannot see it, and the beginner is well advised to learn at least some of the more common ones. To this end one needs to buy a small tape player and a set of bird call tapes of the birds of southern Africa. The most used are those by Len Gillard and those by Guy Gibbon.

In the beginning try to make a list of the birds you know or believe to be in your area, then set about learning their calls. There will probably be about 30 common bird calls you will need to become familiar with, perhaps more during the summer when the migrants are with us, but even if you get to grips with half of that number it will prove most helpful. Play them in the car while driving to the office; it is less likely to drive the family mad.

Some birders collect bird calls by recording them in the field, but it does involve carrying much extra equipment and I don't advise that in the early stages. Recorded bird calls can also be used to entice a bird closer. Sometimes it works and sometimes it doesn't and here a word of warning is appropriate. Should a bird respond to the taped call, switch off the machine immediately and study the bird; please don't drive the creature to distraction by over-playing it. On hearing its call within its home territory a bird will come to find what it thinks to be an intruder: another of its own species that may be attempting to usurp its territory. The bird's reaction will be at its most intense when it is breeding. If the call continues the bird may become frantic in its search for the other bird and may vent its fury on its mate, injuring it or even killing it. I have seen it happen. So if you wish to call birds by tape have regard for their well-being and switch off the cassette once a bird has responded.

CASE STUDY

In your Johannesburg garden you are aware of a small, sparrow-like bird singing sweetly from the top of a tree; you cannot see it well, but later it is feeding in your flower bed and you see that it has bold white eyebrows. What is it?

Step 1: As already noticed, it was sparrow size.

Step 2: On closer inspection you were surprised at its heavy, conical bill.

Step 3: Nothing unusual about its legs, similar to those of a sparrow.

Step 4: Apart from its prominent white eyebrows it was a greyish little bird, but the top of its head was well streaked black on white.

Step 5: The only habitat it has been seen in is the garden.

Step 6: It either sings from the top of the tree or feeds on grass seeds.

A little grey songbird with a bold white eyebrow, streaks on its crown and a very heavy bill. Obviously a seedeater so we start looking at the light green coded pages (between 404 and 443). We find only two sparrow-like birds that have bold white eyebrows, they are the Yellowthroated Sparrow on page 405 and the Streakyheaded Canary on page 439. The only one that is likely to be seen in Johannesburg, and with a streaky crown, is the Streakyheaded Canary on page 439.

LITTLE BROWN JOBS

Otherwise known as LBJs. These are all those small, apparently featureless little brown birds that seem not to have a name. In the beginning you'll hate them; in the end you'll learn to love them, because they do present a challenge. LBJs are reed warblers, cisticolas, larks and pipits, plus all those weavers, bishops, widows and whydahs in non-breeding plumage. Forget them. Pretend they don't exist. Turn your back on them and look at something colourful, that is my advice to the beginner. Don't bite your nails or lose sleep over them, and don't telephone me with your problem LBJs.

When one is at the stage of getting to grips with bird ID there are so many bright, colourful, large birds around that for the first year at least (probably longer) your work will be cut out familiarising yourself with them and their calls. Even without the LBJs you are left with over 800 species, so why jump in at the deep end? Later, when you feel the need for greater challenges, by all means tackle the little brown jobs.

ELBIE JAY

Ornithologicum nightmarensis

PART II

Helpful notes
on specific ID problems

*... should you brave the gales and stagger to the
shoreline or the local pier, you may well be rewarded
by seeing albatrosses ...*

PART II Helpful notes on specific ID problems

Ocean birds. If you live at the coast don't expect to see the birds described between pages 28 and 51 frequently, or even at all unless you are prepared to venture to the seafront whenever a howling gale is blowing, because most of these animals do not venture close inshore under normal conditions. The albatrosses and the related petrels fly best in high winds, soaring in the updrafts created by the windshear caused by high waves. Inshore conditions are normally too calm for them. However, should you brave the gales and stagger to the shoreline or the local pier, you may well be rewarded by seeing albatrosses and some of the larger petrels fairly close inshore. Then you'll have fun trying to ID them while leaning against the wind with freezing hands, wet nose and wet binoculars.

The best way to get to grips with these birds is to go to sea yourself. Several of the coastal bird clubs arrange such trips specifically for seabird-watching. If you don't belong to a bird club you'd best chum up with a local fisherman.

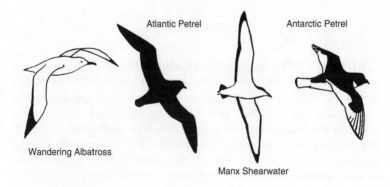

Atlantic Petrel

Antarctic Petrel

Wandering Albatross

Manx Shearwater

Seabirds

On the other hand if you walk along the beach following a period of high winds and storms at sea you may well find seabirds washed ashore - usually, but not always, dead. These wrecked birds are welcomed by the local museums if they are not too badly damaged, and finding and identifying them is exciting in itself. Jackass Penguins (page 29) (and sometimes other penguins too) are frequently found on the beaches, coming ashore to rest or to escape bad conditions.

Gulls and terns. Our gulls (pages 52-5) are scavengers, picking up all sorts of edible fragments found along shorelines and outside beachfront cafés : dead fish, offal, worms, shellfish, toasted sandwiches, you name it. They don't venture far to sea. In fact the Greyheaded Gull is an inland species, frequenting all the great lakes and rivers of Africa and breeding often well away from the sea. We see them on the Natal coast but they have commuted there, probably from the Transvaal where they breed in their thousands at Benoni. Call them gulls, not seagulls.

Gull

Tern

Gulls or terns

Although terns (pages 54-61) are related to gulls they are more slender of wing and more elegant, their flight more buoyant. Most terns live at sea where they make a living following fish shoals, catching their prey by plunge-diving, but they often come to the beaches to rest and can then be seen quite easily. A few of our terns frequent fresh waters. These are the huge Caspian Tern (page 55) which frequents both salt and fresh waters, and the Whiskered and Whitewinged Terns on page 61. These two are known by their square tails whereas most other terns have distinctly forked tails.

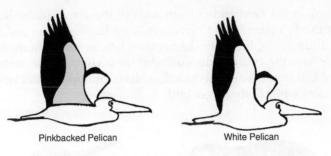

Pinkbacked Pelican   White Pelican

Pinkbacked or White Pelican?

Pelicans. Two pelicans live in southern Africa, the White and the Pinkbacked (page 63). The White Pelican is the largest and whitest and feeds both at sea (especially in Namibia) and in coastal lagoons and rivers. Pelicans are extremely graceful flyers despite their ungainly appearance on land. In flight the White Pelican can be told by its blacker flight feathers. The Pinkbacked Pelican is so named because it has a grey back, or so it seems, because one can't normally see any pink feathers. In fact the Pinkbacked (poor creature) looks a rather grubby pelican.

> Don't believe that story about pelicans flying with their pouches full of fish; it's not true. They use the pouch only as a net with which to catch the fish, which are then swallowed. Fish carried back to their nestlings are carried in the crop and later regurgitated.

Cormorants and the Darter. Of the five cormorants occurring in southern Africa (page 65) two are found regularly on fresh waters. They are the Reed Cormorant and the larger Whitebreasted Cormorant which, however, can also be seen at the coast. The rest are all coastal cormorants and do not venture inland. Cormorants have hooked beaks with which they catch fish and frogs beneath the water, coming to the surface to manipulate and swallow their prey.

Look at the fieldguide illustrations of these two birds. Note that the Whitebreasted Cormorant is by far the larger and, in the adult stage, has only the breast white, whereas immature birds have the entire undersurface of the body white. Immature Reed Cormorants also have dull, whitish underparts, but never the clear white of the larger bird.

Cormorant

Darter

Cormorant or Darter?

The Darter has a more slender, snake-like neck than the cormorants, and habitually swims with only its neck and head out of the water; hence its popular name of Snakebird. It has a sharply pointed, dagger-like bill with which it spears fish under water.

Both cormorants and Darters dry their wings after swimming, perching on some branch or rock where they hold them outspread.

Heron problems. The Blackcrowned Night Heron (page 71), though nocturnal and not easily seen by day, does usually emerge from its reedbed roost towards the late afternoon, and may sit in the open for an hour or so before flying off to work. It's a handsome bird with its white, grey and black plumage, large ruby eyes and white streamers on its nape, but the immature bird is very different, as the fieldguide illustration shows. With its brown-streaked plumage it's frequently mistaken for the larger, rare and secretive Bittern (same page). Don't make this mistake.

TICK BIRD

This name is often wrongly applied to the Cattle Egret (page 72 in the fieldguide), which habitually accompanies feeding cattle and wild ungulates. However, the Cattle Egret's prime purpose in accompanying these animals is to feed on grasshoppers and other insects that are disturbed as the animals graze. Naturally, if the egret were to see a tick on the animal's hide it would peck at it, but the only true tick birds are the oxpeckers (page 388 in the fieldguide) which eat ticks and blowfly larvae as their staple diet.

By the way, bitterns and egrets are all members of the heron family. The identification of the four white egrets (page 73) is a regular problem, but once you've understood a few points it all becomes easy. First, remember that the common Cattle Egret is the white bird you see in the fields in attendance on grazing cattle, buffalo and others. They feed on grasshoppers and other insects disturbed by the animals. They don't feed in water but usually fly to roost above water, and flocks also stand at the water's edge to rest and preen. The Little, Yellowbilled and Great White Egrets are all fish-catchers. The so-called Little Egret (it's bigger than the Cattle Egret!) is told by its black bill and legs plus *yellow feet*. The Yellowbilled Egret is the scarce one. In addition to its yellow bill the upper half of its legs (the tibia) is also dull yellow, the lower half (tarsus) black, while it has a fairly thick neck and quite a few filamentous plumes on its lower neck and back. It's the Great White Egret that causes all the confusion because when it's not breeding (and that's most of the year) its bill is also a rich yellow. *Only for a short period during which mated pairs are courting do they have black bills.* Otherwise its legs and feet are always black.

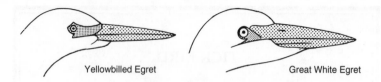

Yellowbilled Egret   Great White Egret

The Yellowbilled Egret's gape ends below the eye,
while the Great White Egret's gape extends behind the eye

So remember that white egrets feeding with cattle in grassland are Cattle Egrets. During the summer, when in breeding condition, Cattle Egrets assume russet coloured plumes on their heads, breasts and backs, while their bills and legs may become quite reddish during courtship.

The Grey Heron and Blackheaded Heron are rather similar (page 75) in both size and plumage colours, but the Grey Heron is a true fisherman and seldom far from water, while the Blackheaded, like the Cattle Egret, *feeds away from water*. The Grey Heron has a white crown and mostly white neck, while its *bill and legs are yellow*. The Blackheaded Heron has the top of the head and most of the neck black (grey in immatures) while the *bill and legs are grey*.

It's also possible to identify these two herons while they are flying (see the fieldguide illustrations): while the Grey Heron's underwings are entirely grey those of the Blackheaded Heron are black and grey.

> Remember that all large herons fly with their necks tucked in; storks and cranes fly with their necks protruding. The exception is the Marabou Stork which does retract its neck in flight.

Large heron

Stork

Crane

Another pair of herons that frequently cause head-scratching are the Purple and Goliath (page 75). The Purple Heron is the smallest heron on the page, being considerably smaller than the Goliath. It has a long, thin, stiletto bill and dark streaks running the length of its slender neck. In contrast the huge Goliath Heron with its rich chestnut and slate-grey plumage has a heavy bill and robust neck. When flying the Goliath flaps its wings ponderously.

Flamingoes. These birds are usually seen in large flocks, sometimes many thousands together. They frequent brackish water from which they extract brine shrimps and microscopic algae. This is done with the head inverted while a pumping action of the tongue draws the water through a series of fine laminae (or comblike teeth) within the bill which filter out these organisms.

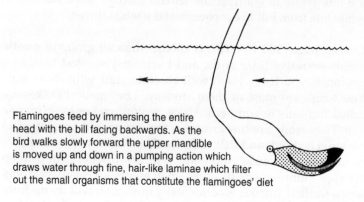

Flamingoes feed by immersing the entire head with the bill facing backwards. As the bird walks slowly forward the upper mandible is moved up and down in a pumping action which draws water through fine, hair-like laminae which filter out the small organisms that constitute the flamingoes' diet

The Greater Flamingo, apart from being the larger of the two, is whiter and has a *pink bill with a black tip*. The very pink Lesser Flamingo has a *deep maroon-red bill with a black tip*; it appears all-black at a distance.

Ducks. Most of our ducks do not present ID problems provided one has a good view of plumage and bill colours, but the female Southern Pochard and Maccoa Duck do; see page 91. The males of both species are distinctive, the pochard with its bronzy-brown plumage, grey bill and red eyes, the Maccoa with black head, chestnut body and brilliant blue bill, and its habit of swimming with its tail erect. Seen at a distance both sexes of either species can be told on jizz alone. The pochards float fairly

The jizz of the female Southern Pochard and a female Maccoa

high on the water, their tails clear of the surface. The Maccoas swim very low in the water with their tails either submerged or held stiffly erect. At close range the head markings of both females give the answer: the pochard with a white crescent shape from the eye to the throat and white around the base of the bill, while in contrast the female Maccoa has a horizontal white line from bill to ear coverts and a white throat.

Crakes, pages 100-103. This is another difficult group of mostly highly secretive little birds, and I seriously suggest that, as a beginner, you leave them well alone to start with. Why not? You won't see most of them anyway. The smallest crakes are called flufftails in southern Africa, pygmy crakes by everyone else. They really are tiny creatures measuring in the region of 15 cm stretched out, and that includes their feet! Most of them live in marshes or dense waterside vegetation where they creep through tunnels made by other small animals. Usually one only sees a flufftail when it is accidentally flushed; it will fly up from one's feet, make off with its legs dangling and drop down a few metres away never to be seen again. Identification of species in these circumstances is largely a matter of guesswork based on habitat and distribution.

The Corncrake, about twice the size of the flufftails, is an uncommon summer visitor from Europe, but can sometimes be flushed while walking through rank grass and lucerne fields. The African Crake also reveals itself occasionally during very wet weather, when it frequents road puddles. The only common, easily seen member of this group is the Black Crake, which occurs on almost all well-vegetated inland pools. Jet black with yellow beak and long red legs, it walks on floating vegetation with its tail cocked upwards. You may tick this one off; it's unmistakable.

CASE STUDY

You were looking at waterbirds in a wetland near Bloemfontein when you noticed a small bird with dull, orange-pink underparts: what could it have been?

Step 1: It was about the size of a sparrow.

Step 2: Its beak was small and slender, blackish in colour.

Step 3: Its legs appeared 'normal' length and were also blackish.

Step 4: Its orange-pink underparts were obvious; it looked like a robin.
Its entire head and upperparts were greyish-brown with no eyebrow present.
When it flew to the ground it showed a white rump and some white in the wings.

Step 5: The habitat was a wetland and the bird was perched on a tall, dry weed.

Step 6: From time to time it would fly down to the ground, seize an insect, and then fly back to a similar perch.

The fact that it was perching on a weed suggests that it was a small passerine of sorts with a slender bill. So it was probably an insect-eater, and perhaps it was a robin. Robins and similar insect-eaters are coded orange-brown. In that section of the fieldguide (pages 316 to 341) nothing in your region has a grey head, no eyebrow, and orange-pink underparts except for no.1 on page 325, and it fits the description exactly: a female Stonechat, the only one of this group that frequents wetlands.

Little grey shorebirds. All the birds shown between pages 109 and 118 (except the jacanas) are generally called 'waders'. They breed in northern Europe, Scandinavia and Siberia, often within the Arctic Circle, and migrate south when they are not breeding. By so doing they escape the rigours of the northern winter. These birds mostly arrive in southern Africa during September-October and depart to their breeding grounds in March-April. A few remain with us during our winter. For the beginner they present a real problem of identification, being basically little grey birds. They frequent the shorelines of inland waters and coastal lagoons, and in some species the seashores, and feed on small organisms in the mud or sand. I prefer to use their American name of 'shorebirds' since it's more descriptive of their behaviour than the term 'waders'. A host of other waterbirds also wade while feeding.

As with the LBJs I would suggest that you avoid shorebirds in the beginning but, should you feel a compulsion to tackle them, then for starters rather concentrate on the seven most common ones. They are, in order of page appearance in the fieldguide:

1. Greenshank, page 108. Compare with Marsh Sandpiper above: the Greenshank is larger (length outstretched 32 cm) and heavier bodied than the Marsh Sandpiper but has similar white underparts, rump and back. Its forehead is white but it has no white eyebrow. It has a rather thick, *slightly upturned blackish bill and greenish or yellowish legs*. It feeds mostly in water, probing beneath the surface. Wary; when flushed it calls a characteristic, triple 'tew-tew-tew'and towers upwards before making off. In flight the white rump and back are distinctive against the wings, which are darkest on the outer panels. Its feet protrude beyond its tail.

2. Marsh Sandpiper, page 108. This and the Greenshank can be confused with each other, so a little caution is needed. *Both have completely white underparts from chin to vent, plus white backs*. Both normally occur singly. The slim-bodied Marsh Sandpiper (length outstretched 23 cm) has a distinct eyebrow and long, slender, *straight* black bill. Its long legs are either dull yellow or greenish-grey. It feeds mostly in shallow water, walking briskly and pecking at the surface. In flight the white rump and back contrast sharply with dark wings; its feet protrude beyond its tail.

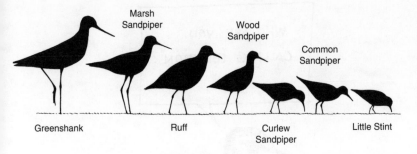

Little grey shore birds

3. Ruff, page 108. These birds often occur in large flocks. Males are noticeably larger than females (30 cm and 24 cm respectively). The characteristic jizz of a feeding, non-breeding Ruff is of a fairly bulky body with a humped back and short, slightly drooped bill. *There is a white patch at the base of the bill*. The adult's legs are orange-yellow (not to be confused with the reddish legs of the rare Redshank, page 117) while those of the immature are dark grey. The feathers of the folded wings are clearly edged in pale buff giving a scaled appearance. The underparts are whitish and there is a mottled greyish patch on the breast. Ruffs feed mostly in shallow waters, sometimes submerging their heads, and in marshlands and damp grasslands. In flight the upper tail coverts show two white, oval patches separated by a dark central line. The feet protrude beyond the tail.

4. Wood Sandpiper, pages 112. This distinctive bird, larger than a sparrow, smaller than a dove (20 cm outstretched) is best told by its grey-brown *upperparts well spotted with white*, its bold white eyebrow and buff-washed breast. The dark bill is straight and about the length of its head; the longish legs greenish-yellow to brownish-yellow. Usually seen singly or in small, loose groups feeding in fresh-water shallows, marshes and moist grasslands; always a few present during winter. When flushed it towers high and calls a shrill 'chiet-chiet' or 'chiff-if-if'. In flight shows a broad white rump and barred upper tail but lacks a wing-bar.

5. Curlew Sandpiper, page 112. Rather larger than a sparrow (19 cm), this very common visitor usually feeds in flocks. The Curlew Sandpiper is best told by its black, *decurved bill* and its longish black legs. There is little of note in its plumage colour-

Common Sandpiper, not as common as its name suggests

ing: white eyebrows and white underparts with a pale grey breast region and grey upperparts. It feeds with its head well down on mud or in shallow waters with bouts of rapid pecking or probing. In flight it shows a broad white rump and white wing-bars.

6. Common Sandpiper, page 112. Not always as common as the name suggests. Slightly larger than a sparrow (20 cm outstretched). A distinctive, mostly solitary bird told by the *constant bobbing of the rear half of its body and the white shoulder-patch* where the white of the underparts wraps around the shoulder. The upperparts are brown, the dark bill about the length of the head, the legs grey-olive. Found on rivers and other quiet waters and normally away from other shorebirds. Feeds out of water as much as in it, with a slow, deliberate action. When flushed calls a shrill 'twee-wee-wee' and *flies low with stiff, downward-bowed wings with a sporadic flicking action.*

7. Little Stint, page 110. A very small shorebird, about the size of a sparrow. Feeds in shallows near the shoreline with a head-down, humpbacked appearance while pecking rapidly. In flocks or singly. The bill is short and fairly thick, this and the shortish legs black. Upperparts grey, eyebrow and underparts white, the breast with an indistinct grey wash. On take-off it calls a sharp 'chit' or rippling 'chitchitchit'. The flight is rapid but thin white wing-bars are visible. The feet do not protrude.

SPOTS, STRIPES AND BARS

The undersides of many birds have distinctive markings such as spots and stripes and, when these terms are used in the fieldguide, they sometimes give rise to confusion. For your guidance the following terms and their usage are applied to appropriate illustrated examples in the fieldguide:

1. Spotted: see Little Spotted Woodpecker on page 271.

2. Barred: see female Black Cuckooshrike on page 299.

3. Striped or streaked: see the Greater Striped Swallow on page 229.

4. Blotched: see Ayre's Eagle (b) on page 167.

5. Banded: see undertail and underwing of Honey Buzzard, page 173.

6. Scalloped: see upperparts of Crested Barbet on page 265.

Wattled and Whitecrowned Plovers. Most plovers are distinctive and easily identified but these two are a frequent cause of confusion; see page 122. Look at the fieldguide illustrations: it is obvious that the only similarities are their yellow beaks, legs and wattles (those dangling things hanging from the base of their bills). The problem is that whereas the Wattled Plover is a fairly common and widely distributed waterside bird the Whitecrowned has a very limited distribution, and is not often seen by most people. When it is seen for the first time one is inclined to jump to the wrong conclusion. Remember that the Wattled Plover is basically greyish-brown, *including its breast and most of its belly,* whereas the Whitecrowned Plover has the *entire top of the head and the entire underparts white.* It also shows a black patch on the folded wing while its wattles are very long. Look for this one on rivers with extensive sandbanks, especially the Levuvhu and Olifants Rivers in the Kruger National Park, and the Chobe River in Botswana.

Difficult little bustards. The bustards are a group of cryptically coloured, terrestrial birds that frequent dry grasslands, and are typified by long legs, longish necks, substantial bodies and flattish heads. They range from about the size of a guineafowl to the huge Kori Bustard which is smaller only than the Ostrich and is our heaviest flying bird. In southern Africa the smaller bustards are called korhaans and, since a number of them have black bellies in one or other of the sexes, there is much confusion about their identities. The culprits are the Redcrested and Black Korhaans (page 132) and the Blackbellied Korhaan (page 136).

The Redcrested Korhaan is so called because it doesn't have a red crest, or at least it doesn't appear to have. In fact, only the male has this crest, which is a sort of brick-red colour, and he only reveals it when courting. At other times he tucks it away and you will look for it in vain. Both sexes have black bellies. This is a bushveld korhaan and is plentiful in the Kruger Park, its shrill call being heard daily. Like all korhaans it walks slowly and can be examined at close range from a motor car. What clinches it for ID purposes are the creamy *arrow-shaped marks all over the upperpart of its body.* Now check the fieldguide illustration.

The Black and Whitequilled Korhaans are grassland or Karoo species and are just about indistinguishable in the field unless

*Korhaans walk very slowly so they can
easily be examined from your car*

one sees a male in flight, when the presence or absence of white wing-quills is evident. However, their respective ranges are mutually exclusive, and so there is no need to chase them into the air. Whereas the males are quite distinctive the females, with black only on their bellies, are sometimes recorded erroneously as Blackbellied Korhaans (see below). In fact the ranges of these two species are just about exclusive. However, for ID purposes note that the females of the Black or Whitequilled Korhaans have their *upperparts pale beige with black, transverse barring*, and their bills are pink with whitish tips.

The Blackbellied Korhaan was named by a male chauvinist because the female has a white belly. This species has the alternative name of Longlegged Korhaan, and this is a good field feature, its legs being comparatively longer and slimmer than those of other korhaans of similar size. It is a grassland species. Note that the *black of the male's belly extends up its throat to its chin and around its ear coverts*. When these features are noted, and the fieldguide illustrations carefully compared, there should be no cause for confusion between this and the previous species.

Francolin

Guineafowls

Francolin

Francolin or guineafowl?

Francolins. With francolins, as with most other birds, get to know those that occur in the region where you are birding: it is unlikely that there will be more than three or four species. Become familiar with the jizz and calls of those around you. Outside of national parks francolins tend to be shy, running or flying off at the first sign of a human, and one's opportunities of examining them are few in such circumstances. However, even when a francolin is running away it is usually possible to note its leg colour, and that's halfway to identifying it. In the Kruger Park, for example, there are only five common francolins, and getting to know them is not difficult since they are not only accustomed to motor cars but also frequent rest camps.

Swainson's and Rednecked Francolins, page 144. Swainson's is perhaps the most common and widespread of them all. Told by its *black legs* and red facial and throat skin, it is sometimes confused with the Rednecked Francolin which also has red skin around its head but has *red legs*. If one looks at the distribution maps for these two species it will be seen that their ranges are virtually exclusive, the Rednecked being more easterly while Swainson's extends westwards into Namibia. The voices of these two birds are not dissimilar, being a series of harsh crowing sounds, but that of the Rednecked is the less harsh of the two and tends to be rendered in longer sequences. Listen to a bird tape if possible.

Crested Francolin, page 142. This is the most distinctive of all from its habit of *holding its tail cocked like a bantam chicken*. Its markings too are distinctive: reddish legs, a dark crown, white eyebrow, a well-spotted throat and upper breast. Its squeaky 'beer and cognac' call is usually heard well before dawn. This is a bushveld species, being absent from grasslands, karoo and much of the arid west.

Redbilled Francolin, page 142. Throughout the Kalahari and much of Namibia the Redbilled is the common francolin. This bird of the semi-arid regions is tame and approachable in most areas. The red bill and legs, and the yellow ring about the eye, are diagnostic.

Cape Francolin, page 142. This large francolin is confined to the southern and western Cape, where it is common. It has dull reddish legs and a streaky underbody, but appears all-dark at a distance. Its high-pitched cackling call carries far and then fades.

Natal Francolin, page 146. In spite of its name this bird occurs as far north as Zambia. Red legs and a red bill with a yellow base, plus habitat are the best guides for identifying this species. Coveys of up to ten birds are found on wooded riverbanks, rocky hillsides and in wooded valleys where their loud cackling call is heard particularly in the mornings and evenings.

White-throated francolins. These are the Greywing, Orange River, Shelley's and Redwing Francolins, and the group is so named for its members' distinctive throat markings. All have dull yellow legs but specific identity can sometimes be a problem. With these four it is essential to refer to the distribution maps, habitat descriptions and calls.

Greywing Francolin, page 144. This species occurs only from the Drakensberg to the western Cape, and is found mostly in mountain grasslands and the foothills. Its throat is whitish well speckled with black.

Orange River Francolin, page 146. Occurs in the southern Transvaal, Orange Free State, northern Cape, Botswana and northern Namibia. A variable species, being palest in the west. Could easily be confused with the Redwing Francolin but their ranges are mutually exclusive.

Redwing Francolin, page 146. From the southern Transvaal southward to inland Natal and the southern seaboard. The distribution does not overlap with that of either Shelley's or Orange River Francolins.

Shelley's Francolin, page 146. Closely similar to the Orange River Francolin. The distributions of this and both the Orange River and Redwing Francolins are mutually exclusive. A bushveld and grassland species, it has a shrill, crowing call which sounds like 'I'll drink yer beer' repeated several times.

Coqui Francolin may take several minutes to cross a road

Coqui Francolin, page 142. These little francolins are partridge-like in their behaviour in that they don't run away but freeze, and only flush when about to be stepped on. Note the sexual differences (sexual dimorphism). In nature reserves, on encountering a motor car, they walk extremely slowly and may take several minutes to cross the road. The common call of the Coqui Francolin, usually heard long before the birds are seen, is a squeaky 'be-kwik, be-kwik, be-kwik', while the male also has a shrill, crowing call given in a descending cadence.

CASE STUDY

You are in the Kalahari Gemsbok National Park when you see a small, pale-coloured plover-like bird running about near a pan: what is it?

Step 1: Definitely larger than a sparrow, perhaps about dove size but quite a different shape to a dove.

Step 2: Its beak is short, pointed and black.

Step 3: It has long legs like some plovers, but this one's legs are white.

Step 4: The bird is very pale, almost white, but it has two blackish bands encircling its breast and lower neck; its wings seem to be dappled with black and white.

Step 5: It frequents the dry ground near the pan, but has not been seen to drink and doesn't appear to mind the midday sun.

Step 6: It feeds on open, stony ground, runs about very quickly then suddenly stops and jerks its head back.

Since the bird looks and behaves like a plover let's look at the group coded red, which includes plovers on pages 121 to 127. There are some whitish, long-legged birds on page 127, but none with two blackish breast-bands. In fact there are several long-legged terrestrial birds in this section of the book, so let's page over slowly. Suddenly, on page 131, we have it: the Doublebanded Courser. Description, habitat and location all fit.

RECOGNISING RAPTORS IN FLIGHT

Getting to know the wing shapes and flight jizz of birds of prey is the key to speedy familiarity with the various groups. (Silhouettes are not to scale)

VULTURES

EAGLES

BUZZARDS

LARGE KITES

HARRIERS

FALCONS

KESTRELS

GOSHAWKS and SPARROWHAWKS

Vultures. The Cape and Whitebacked Vultures (page 152) are two superficially similar species. The larger Cape Vulture is most common in mountains where it breeds on high cliffs, but at other times it wanders over a wide area. The Whitebacked Vulture (you can't often see the white back) is a bird of the bushveld and woodlands where it nests in trees, and is therefore common in many national parks.

Cape Vultures become very pale with age, their bare skin a deep reddish-purple, their *eyes honey coloured*. Young birds have browner plumage, their bare skin more reddish. The Whitebacked Vulture generally looks darker than the Cape although old birds do tend to get paler, and the white back is only present in mature birds. Its *eyes are dark brown* and the bare skin deep purple to blackish. In flight they look very similar, but the Cape Vulture shows *pale secondary wing feathers towards the body*.

True eagles and snake eagles, pages 162-9. Among all the birds of prey only *true eagles have their legs fully feathered to the toes*. The specialised snake eagles, like buzzards, harriers, goshawks, falcons and others, *have the lower part of their legs (the tarsus) unfeathered*.

Snake eagles (pages 158-61) can usually be told by their loosely feathered heads which give them a bulbous-headed appearance and by their large, yellow, owl-like eyes. Snake eagles also have short toes that enable them to grip a snake and kill it by crushing; in this action long toes would be an impediment. The Bateleur and the African Fish Eagle (page 168) are probably aberrant snake eagles.

Brown eagles. Birds of prey generally are a notoriously difficult group to get to grips with, and not only for the beginner: most people struggle with them. For one thing many brown eagles look alike and, for another, young birds usually have different plumages to adults. Since some of the large eagles take from five to seven years to reach breeding maturity the growing bird can go through at least two plumage changes before assuming its final, adult one. As examples of this see the Bateleur and the Blackbreasted Snake Eagle (page 161) and the Crowned Eagle (page 167). These illustrations need to be studied carefully by the *ab initio* raptorphile. Initially however, your main battle will be with the brown eagles, and you'll probably snap your fieldguide closed and say one brown eagle looks like another. Not true. Let's look at the eight chief offenders.

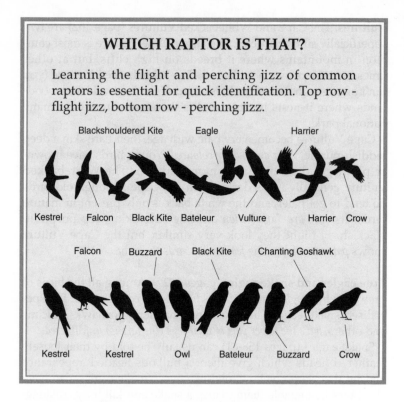

WHICH RAPTOR IS THAT?

Learning the flight and perching jizz of common raptors is essential for quick identification. Top row - flight jizz, bottom row - perching jizz.

Blackshouldered Kite   Eagle   Harrier

Kestrel   Falcon   Black Kite   Bateleur   Vulture   Harrier   Crow

Falcon   Buzzard   Black Kite   Chanting Goshawk

Kestrel   Kestrel   Owl   Bateleur   Buzzard   Crow

1. Immature Bateleur, page 160. Because the adult Bateleur is such a striking bird one tends to forget that the juvenile is plain brown. But note its bulky, Bateleur-type body, extremely short tail, bulbous-looking head and bare legs. No other brown eagle has the Bateleur jizz.

2. Brown Snake Eagle, page 160. Completely dark brown, occasionally with a few white under-feathers showing on the body during moult. Otherwise a typical snake eagle with its bulbous head, large yellow eyes and bare legs. This species is a still-hunter, perching erect on top of a tree from where it watches the ground for its prey, and its *upright jizz* is diagnostic.

3. Booted Eagle, page 162. This is a very small eagle, larger than a pigeon, smaller than a guineafowl. (What a comparison!) It comes in two plumages: completely dark brown or with a white breast. It's the dark brown one that causes the head-scratching. Look for the *white patches at the shoulders* (where wings meet

body); these are visible both when the bird is perched and when flying, at which time they look like aircraft landing lights. Also when the Booted Eagle is flying, if you can see its upper wings, note the paler wing coverts (see the fieldguide illustration); this upperwing pattern is shared only by the *Milvus* kites (page 158) and they can be told by their forked tails anyway.

A plain brown eagle with stove-pipe trousers

4. Lesser Spotted Eagle, page 162. This is a non-breeding summer visitor so you won't see it between April and September. A plain brown eagle with *stove-pipe trousers*. (Other true eagles have baggy pants.) The slender legs are present in both the adult and immature, the latter also showing the white wing-spots. This species can often be seen in flocks, feeding on flying termites as they emerge from their burrows, or raiding breeding colonies of Redbilled Queleas (page 404). In flight the Lesser Spotted Eagle appears surprisingly heavy-winged for a small eagle.

5. Wahlberg's Eagle, (page 162). Another summer visitor, but this one breeds. Wahlberg's Eagles arrive in August/September and immediately set about repairing their nests from the previous summer; so, since all other eagles breed during winter, *any summer breeding brown eagle is a Wahlberg's*. This is another small eagle, only a little larger than the Booted, and it also comes in both brown and white-bodied forms, the dark being either very dark or medium brown. There are few distinguishing features in a perched, all-dark Wahlberg's, except that its head is long and this, coupled with a prominent bill, gives it a characteristic *long-headed jizz*. The head also shows a small crest when the breeze lifts the crown feathers and, in all but the very dark form, it is possible to see a *distinct darkening around the eye recess*.

6. Longcrested Eagle, page 164. This brown eagle is mercifully adorned with a ludicrous crest at all ages, so here's one easy ID.

THE FASTEST

It is generally accepted that the Peregrine Falcon is the swiftest interceptor of all predatory birds, immobilising its prey in a spectacular, headlong dive called a 'stoop'. During the stoop a Peregrine may reach a speed of 250-380 km/h, striking its quarry, usually a flying pigeon-size bird, with split-second timing, either decapitating the victim or stunning it. The falcon then executes a swift turnabout and grabs the hapless bird as it falls.

7 & 8. Steppe and Tawny Eagles, page 164. The Steppe Eagle is a non-breeding summer visitor, with us from late October to February. Adults are large, *very dark brown* eagles with baggy pants and, usually, a russet patch on the nape. Tawny Eagles are never as dark as the adult Steppe. In contrast immature Steppe Eagles are very similar to the Tawny Eagle, and can be very pale in colour. Steppe Eagles may be seen in flocks feeding on flying termites like the Lesser Spotted Eagle, and may mix with that species. The important thing to look for in the Steppe Eagle, at all ages, is the *prominent orange-yellow gape that extends backwards to a point level with the back of the eye.*

The resident Tawny Eagle can be seen in darker and lighter tones of brown in addition to the more regular tawny colour (see fieldguide illustrations), but when there is doubt as to whether you are looking at this or the immature Steppe Eagle, note that the Tawny has a yellow (not orange-yellow) *gape which extends back only to a point level with the centre of its eye*, its paler colour making it less prominent than the gape of the Steppe.

Small accipiters. 'Accipiter' is a collective name for sparrowhawks and goshawks. On page 176 of the fieldguide are four little grey accipiters that are notorious for the headaches they cause. Although their sizes range from 25 cm to 40 cm this is not always evident in the field. These birds are very shy, alert and swift of flight. They frequent woodlands. Usually when one is spotted in a tree it takes off away from you and flies to the next tree, and will continue like this all the time you follow it. One's only hope of getting a reasonable view of a perched accipiter is from a motor car. There is some hope, however, since they normally tend to fly low and turn to left or right, at which time one can snatch a brief view of its upperparts, and that's what you need.

In the Little Sparrowhawk the upper tail shows two white spots plus a narrow white tip: diagnostic. In the Little Banded Goshawk the upperparts are plain grey: diagnostic. In the Gabar Goshawk one sees a broad white rump: diagnostic. In the Ovambo Sparrowhawk the upper tail shows three pale bands traversed by two pale feather-shafts: diagnostic but difficult to see.

Harriers, pages 180-83. Remember that harriers are long-winged, long-tailed raptors that are seen over marshes or grass-lands. They fly low with leisurely wing beats, their heads looking downward and their legs hanging slightly below the horizontal. Harriers settle on the ground rather than perch. They also nest on the ground.

Kestrels, pages 190-93. These pages show the Greater, Lesser and Rock Kestrels. All three have similar reddish-brown plumages and give rise to a certain amount of confusion. The Greater and Rock Kestrels are resident species and both may be commonly seen perched on roadside telephone poles. The adult Greater Kestrel has *whitish eyes* (dusky in the immature), the Rock Kestrel *dark brown eyes*. Rock Kestrels habitually hover when hunting; Greater Kestrels do this less often. The more slender Lesser Kestrel, by contrast, is a non-breeding summer visitor with us from October to March only and normally occurs in flocks that often forage from telephone and power lines.

Greater Kestrels *never* have grey heads. They are tawny all over, lightly streaked blackish on the underparts, heavily barred blackish on the upperparts. In flight the underwings are whitish, the tail barred in light brown.

Rock Kestrels usually have grey heads, darker or even lacking in females. The general body colouring is a *rich chestnut*. The male has a grey tail with a broad black subterminal bar; the female has several black bars. In flight the underwings are whitish, well spotted and barred with black.

Male Lesser Kestrels have blue-grey heads (not throats), wing-bars and tails, the tail with a broad black subterminal bar. The back is a rich chestnut colour. The underwings are whitish. The female Lesser Kestrel has paler chestnut upperparts than the male, while the underparts are creamy, well streaked with black; only the throat is unmarked. In flight the underwings are well spotted with black.

DID YOU KNOW?

That owls, falcons and kestrels build no nest of their own? Instead they lay their eggs on a bare cliff ledge, a natural tree cavity or the disused nest of another bird of prey. Sometimes they use man-made structures such as balconies and gutters.

Ringnecked doves. Since they are very common few birders pay any real attention to these doves. The three in question are on page 196 of my fieldguide and, although each has a black half-collar on its hind neck, there are some subtle differences, both in plumage and call.

The Cape Turtle Dove (smaller than a city pigeon) is equally widespread in suburbia and the semi-desert while its harsh 'work harder, work harder' call is well known. Its head and body are pale grey, its wings darker.

The larger Redeyed Dove (same size as the city pigeon) is absent from the dry west and has a wider collar than the Cape Turtle Dove; *it has a red iris surrounded by a dark red fleshy eye-ring and its body plumage is tinged pink.* Its well-known call is 'coo-coo, coo-kuk-cuk-coo' or 'Father, why don't you work?' Some say the bird is calling its own name 'I am a Redeyed Dove'.

The Mourning Dove is somewhere between the other two in size and is found only in the north-eastern Transvaal, including the Kruger National Park, along the Zambezi River and in the

Okavango Delta of Botswana. It is distinguished by a *grey head, pinkish breast, and a yellow iris with a red eye-ring*. Its call is a soft 'kur-r-r-r-r'.

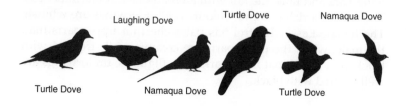

Turtle Dove   Laughing Dove   Turtle Dove   Namaqua Dove

Turtle Dove   Namaqua Dove   Turtle Dove

The jizz of some doves

Wood doves. There are three small wood doves in southern Africa. They are the Namaqua Dove (page 196), Bluespotted and Emeraldspotted Doves (page 200). What tells us that these are wood doves? The fact that when flying they reveal *chestnut-brown wings and double black bars across their backs*.

BROOD PARASITES

A brood parasite is a bird that lays its eggs in the nest of another, host species, and takes no part in the rearing of its young. Can you name four groups of brood parasites in southern Africa?

Cuckoos, pages 208-12; Honeyguides, pages 272-4; Whydahs and Widow-finches, pages 432-4; Cuckoo Finch (or parasitic weaver), page 430.

Green cuckoos, page 208. The Klaas's and Diederik Cuckoos are closely similar, more so the males, while the forest-loving Emerald Cuckoo is markedly different: the male has yellow underparts and the female is well banded. Since both Klaas's and Diederik Cuckoos are widespread in urban areas during the summer months confusion reigns. Perhaps the most important difference is their eye colours: dark in Klaas's and red with a red eye-ring in the Diederik. Both males have glossy green upperparts, *Klaas's with a small white spot behind the eye, Diederik with a full white eyebrow*. Diederik has, in addition, more white spots and feather margins on its wings. The female Diederik has more bronzy-green upperparts while the female Klaas's, being well banded, could be confused with the female Emerald Cuckoo except for its green (not bronze) wings. Young, newly fledged Diederik Cuckoos have coral-pink beaks and blue eyes.

Look-alike grey cuckoos. On page 211 we see four very similar grey cuckoos, one of which is the well known (or much heard) Redchested Cuckoo, better known as the Piet-my-vrou. All four are with us only in summer and no. 4, the Lesser Cuckoo, is so rare that you may as well forget about it. Of the three remaining grey cuckoos the Piet-my-vrou makes its presence known in gardens almost everywhere between October and January but, since it usually calls from the top of a tall tree, it's seldom seen. The European Cuckoo (no. 2) is the bird that sings 'cuckoo' during the European summer and then comes south to enjoy our summer; females of this species *sometimes* have a rusty collar resembling the rusty chest of no. 1. The African Cuckoo (no. 3) is a resident species that closely resembles no. 2, in fact the only real difference is in their bill colours; compare the fieldguide illustrations.

Since these three cuckoos are so confusingly similar I recommend that you become acquainted with the calls of the Redchested and the African Cuckoos, since the European Cuckoo doesn't call at all while in Africa. The 'Piet-my-vrou' call of the Redchested Cuckoo is well enough known to need no description. That of the African Cuckoo is rather like 'cuckoo' backwards: the male calls a soft 'coo-cuck'. It's a bird of woodlands.

Look-alike coucals, page 214. Senegal, Copperytailed and Burchell's Coucals are indeed very similar in both appearance and call. Since the distinctively marked Whitebrowed Coucal (previously considered a race of Burchell's) has now been given its rightful status as a full species it presents no problems. The three remaining species have mutually exclusive distributions over most of southern Africa with the exception of the Okavango region of Botswana where Senegal and Copperytailed live together.

The Copperytailed is larger than the Senegal (44-50 cm and 41 cm respectively) and, as its name implies, the large tail has a distinct coppery tinge while the mantle is darker; see fieldguide illustrations. To simplify the matter then: coucals south of the Limpopo will be Burchell's; those that look like Burchell's north of the Limpopo will be Senegal, except in the Okavango where you have to determine whether they are Senegal or Copperytailed, as both occur.

Owls. Most owls are little known because of their nocturnal lifestyles. However, there are two medium-large owls that live in grasslands and can sometimes be seen by day. They both frequent moist vleis and the edges of reedbeds where the grass is long and matted. They are the Marsh and Grass Owls (page 216), and the two are very different in appearance. The Marsh Owl is often hunting or merely sunning itself in the mornings until about 09h00, and again in the late afternoons when it sits on fence posts or flies around. If flushed the Marsh Owl will fly about over you, and then its distinctive chestnut coloured wing panels can be seen; see the fieldguide illustrations.

The Grass Owl is less easily seen but when disturbed it will take off and fly away, settling at some distance away. This behaviour alone gives the clue to its ID in contrast to that of the Marsh Owl. Should you come across a nest of Grass Owl chicks the young birds, and the adult too if it stands its ground, will hiss at you, and this can be quite scary.

Eagle Owls (page 220) are merely our larger owls, they are not related in any way to eagles. Perhaps the most common and widespread is the Spotted Eagle Owl which is found in a wide variety of habitats, including suburbia. If you have in town heard a soft hooting at night it will be this bird. Spotted Eagle Owls like large trees, often bluegums, and emerge for the night's hunting at twilight when they perch on rooftops and gate posts. They also live on rocky hillsides. All three eagle owls have ear tufts which are not ears at all but feather adornments. Let's see how the three owls compare.

The Spotted Eagle Owl has *pale yellow eyes* and finely barred underparts. If you should approach it by day while it is perched it will, in common with many other owls, sleek its plumage and almost close its eyes.

*Walking too close to a nest of Grass Owl chicks
can be a little scary*

The Cape Eagle Owl is much less common than the Spotted and doesn't venture into suburbia. It frequents hillside valleys with rocks at the upper end or grasslands with rocky outcrops and trees. The Cape Eagle Owl is larger than the Spotted Eagle Owl, it has *chrome-yellow to orange eyes* and its underparts are more heavily blotched and barred; its call is also deeper than that of the Spotted Eagle Owl.

The Giant Eagle Owl, largest of the three, is a bird of bushveld and the larger trees along rivers. It can sometimes be seen perched during the day when its diagnostic features are its *pink eyelids and dark eyes*. It has a grunting call.

Nightjars. This is one of the most difficult group of birds to ID, mainly because their plumages are so similar. Apart from the male Pennantwinged Nightjar with its long wing-pennants, should you see it, the rest have dappled brown plumage. What's more, since they only start flying at dusk they are seldom encountered during the day unless almost trodden on while at roost on the ground. However, there are a few clues in such cases.

Should you flush a nightjar by day first check the distribution maps to see which one is likely to be where you are. If it is summertime, and if you have seen a dark coloured nightjar lying lengthwise along a branch, it is most likely to be a European Nightjar. If you have flushed one from the ground (usually under a tree) it will probably be either a Rufouscheeked, Fierynecked or Mozambique Nightjar. If the bird has been flushed from rocks most likely it will be the Freckled Nightjar. Note that the Natal Nightjar occurs only on the Natal coast and in northern Botswana.

Usually when a roosting nightjar has been flushed it will settle again not far away. Watch it settle then creep quietly to within a few metres and examine the bird with binoculars. By far the best way to become familiar with nightjars is to learn their calls. Also, since they habitually sit in roads after dark, they are frequent road casualties. An examination of the bird's wing and tail spots, coupled with the charts on pages 226-7 in the fieldguide, will help to establish its identity.

DID YOU KNOW?

Most birds that nest in holes or cavities lay white eggs. In southern Africa they include the Greyrumped and Saw-winged Swallows, Brownthroated, Banded, and House Martins, all the bee-eaters, kingfishers, rollers, hornbills, barbets, woodpeckers and honeyguides. Most owls also lay white eggs.

Striped swallows, page 228. The Greater Striped Swallow is so named because it's larger than the Lesser Striped Swallow, not because it has larger stripes. In fact it has thinner stripes and less of them whereas the Lesser has an abundance of heavy stripes. Another way to tell them is by the extent of chestnut colouring on their heads: whereas the Greater has its ear coverts white, *in the Lesser the colouring extends over the ear coverts.*

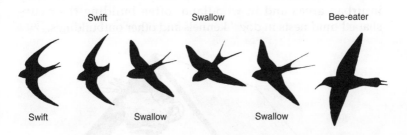

Swift, swallow or bee-eater?

Blue swallows. The four swallows on page 232 often cause confusion. They all have steel-blue upperparts and white underparts while two have some orange colouring on their heads. These swallows all have soft twittering calls. Let's look at them a bit closer: European Swallows (which are also known as Barn Swallows in America and elsewhere) are, as their name suggests, visiting migrants from Europe; they do not breed here. Arriving in September they are by far the most numerous swallow in our skies until their departure in March, at which time they can be seen gathering on telephone wires prior to their long journey.

European Swallows usually feed in flocks, often mixing with other swallows and with swifts. On arrival here they will be seen with long tail-streamers, but these soon drop as the birds enter their moulting phase. So for much of our summer they will be seen without tail-streamers until new ones grow in the new year. In flight they appear to have blackish heads and throats; in fact their foreheads and throats are brick red while a blackish band separates the throat from the breast. Since European Swallows breed just prior to coming south one sees many juvenile birds in their much duller plumage: see the field-guide.

Wiretailed Swallows are seldom far from water, in pairs, usually near river bridges, dam walls and buildings near water, and build their cup-shaped mud nests on these structures or on rocks. This swallow is identified by its *entirely orange cap*, immaculate white underparts and wire-like tail-streamers.

Pearlbreasted Swallows are identified by blue upperparts, white underparts and *lack of tail-streamers*. Although this is a resident species within our region it is present in many areas only during summer. Pairs are sparsely distributed, occurring in urban areas and in woodland, often building their cup-shaped mud nests in dogs' kennels and other outbuildings.

Greyrumped Swallows have grey-brown rumps and caps of the same colour. However, the grey rump frequently becomes very faded so that in flight the birds may appear white-rumped, then they can be confused with the migrant House Martin (page 236). Perhaps the most interesting thing about Greyrumped Swallows is that they nest underground in rodent burrows or in the nest holes of bee-eaters in banks. Active colonies can often be found in riverbanks, at other times in fields.

CASE STUDY

You are in the Kruger Park and have seen a small bird with some yellow on it: what is it?

Step 1: It was definitely smaller than a sparrow; like a white-eye.

Step 2: Its beak appeared blackish; it was short and slender.

Step 3: Its legs were 'normal' length (like a sparrow's), and greyish.

Step 4: Its upperparts were grey-brown, the chin and breast paler, but its underbelly was pale yellow. There was a faint stripe through its eye.

Step 5: The bird was in a small, dry bush.

Step 6: It was feeding in the outer branches, pecking at aphids.

Since this small bird had a short, slender beak, it was either a warbler or a flycatcher. Because of its active behaviour most likely a warbler. Its yellow underbelly is the clue; not many like this.

Use the key to the colour coding on page ix to find that the group of birds which includes warblers is coded magenta. Turn to the magenta section of the book and start looking at warblers from page 332.

Several seem to have pale yellow underparts but their sizes seem too large. What's this on page 344? It has a pale yellow belly and greyish-brown upperparts; it also has a paler throat and breast plus the line through the eye. — You've got it! It's a Yellowbellied Eremomela, often seen in the Kruger Park.

DID YOU KNOW?

A pair of Hamerkops take several weeks to build their huge, domed nest and, according to my own observations, they work only from dawn until about 8 am each day. The nest is placed on either a tree or a rock, not far from water, and is built of sticks, reeds, mud and various debris. It has a single, central chamber which is reached by an entrance hole placed low on the side of the nest that protrudes into space; in this way no mammalian predator can gain entrance. However, this does not prevent other birds from gaining entrance to this most desirable residence, and barn owls especially are keen contenders. In many cases the owls move in before the rightful owners, leaving the poor Hamerkops no choice but to start afresh elsewhere. Egyptian Geese also favour Hamerkop nests, usually laying their eggs in a depression on the top, which results in the inner nest chamber caving-in.

Martins, pages 234-7. Martins are a kind of swallow with squarish, as opposed to forked, tails. Most martins have brown colouring whereas swallows are dark blue; the single exception is the migrant House Martin which has blue upperparts like a swallow.

Swifts, pages 239-43. Swifts differ from swallows in many ways and are in no way related. First, *swifts cannot perch*, they can only cling to rocks and walls. Swifts are mostly dark brown and appear black in the air, although some have white rumps or underparts. Not all swifts have forked tails; the common Little Swift and the spinetailed swifts have square tails. Swifts mostly fly faster than swallows and flap their wings faster. Many swifts have taken to breeding under freeway fly-overs, river bridges and the eaves of highrise buildings.

Kingfishers. On page 252 are two similar brown birds, the Brownhooded and Striped Kingfishers. In spite of their names neither is a fisherman, they live instead in woodlands and eat insects. As kingfishers go they are both dull, having blue only on part of their wings, their backs and tails. The Brownhooded Kingfisher can also be found in well-wooded suburbia, perching on a low branch. This species is much larger than the Striped Kingfisher and has a large, *all-red bill*. Its call is a loud, descending 'kik, kik-kik-kik-kik-kik'. The much smaller Striped Kingfisher gets its name from the streaks on its crown, not always easily seen because it usually perches high up on a tree. Its underparts are whiter than those of the Brownhooded, and its bill is *dark above and red below*. The call, a duet between the sexes, is a far-carrying 'trrrrr, deeeoo, deeeoo, deeeoo'.

Also on page 252 are two colourful small kingfishers, the Pygmy and the Malachite, the first an insect-eater, the second a fisherman. The Pygmy Kingfisher is normally a woodland species but sometimes plunges into streams, perhaps to catch insects or to bathe. While the colouring of the two is similar note that the Pygmy has a blue crown *that does not touch the eyes*; it also has a violet wash on the side of its head. The more common Malachite Kingfisher has a turquoise crown *that touches its eyes*; it lacks a violet wash on its head. Look for it on streams and ponds.

Woodpeckers, page 268. At first glance the four common woodpeckers on this page look very much alike despite the various amounts of red on their heads, but there are easy ways of identifying them. Head markings can sometimes prove confusing whereas comparative sizes and the markings of the birds' underparts provide a foolproof guide to identities. The smallest woodpecker is the Cardinal (14-16 cm), next largest is the Goldentailed (20-23 cm), then comes Bennett's (22-24 cm) and finally the Bearded (25 cm). Both Cardinal and Goldentailed Woodpeckers have streaked underparts, the Cardinal with the heavier streaking; this plus their distinctive head markings should clinch it. Bennett's Woodpecker has spotted underparts and the Bearded has banded underparts.

Larks, pages 276-87. Yet another confusing group: these are little brown grass birds. 'They all look the same and how can I tell them from pipits anyway?' How often I've heard this tale of woe! Look at any page of larks in the fieldguide and rest assured that never more than a handful of them will occur in your region or the region you are visiting. The rest are put there to fox you. First, and I stress this, examine the distribution maps. You'll probably find the one you've 'seen' doesn't even occur where you think it is! If you live in the western Cape for example there can only be five lark species and one finchlark in your region, and the same applies to many other regions. So take heart, the larks are really not as bad as they appear.

There are small larks and larger ones. There are those that sing from the tops of bushes, those that sing in the air and a lot that don't sing much anywhere. There are those with short bills and those with long ones; studied carefully every lark has something going for it. So study the maps, isolate the few you are likely to see, study their plumage (if they'll let you), note their behaviour and jizz.

Larks that sing from a bush top are the Melodious, Sabota, Fawncoloured, Rufousnaped and Shortclawed Larks. Of these the Melodious, Sabota and Rufousnaped are the more common and regular songsters. The Fawncoloured has a westerly, largely dry-region distribution, while the Shortclawed has a very limited distribution in the north-western Transvaal and Botswana.

The larger larks (sparrow size or larger) that sing in the air are the Flappet, Clapper, Redcapped, Spikeheeled, Thickbilled and Longbilled Larks. The smaller ones (smaller than a sparrow) with aerial songs are Rudd's (rare and very localised), Botha's (ditto) and Pinkbilled Larks. Sclater's, Stark's and Gray's Larks all belong to the dry west so you won't see them unless you make a special trip. Much the same applies to the Dune and Red Larks while the Karoo Lark is similarly isolated.

The little finchlarks (smaller than a sparrow) (page 288) usually occur in flocks. Ignore the females, look at the males: two have white ear-patches, one an additional white crown-patch, the other no white at all.

Pipits. I once knew a man who had made a close study of pipits over many years and, in discussion with me, he said that if anyone claimed to be able to identify the various pipits in the field such a person was either extremely clever or a liar. That at least tends to sum up those pipits illustrated on page 289 of my fieldguide. If you can say 'It's a pipit' you've made good progress but, as a beginner, leave them for sunnier days. The colourful longclaws, which are pipits of sorts, are easily identified, as are the related wagtails.

Drongoes and other black birds. On page 297 of my fieldguide I have illustrated four similar all-black birds. In so doing I have put members of three different families all on one page, and have seriously rocked the ornithological boat. Such goings-on are considered outrageous! So be it. The idea is to help the beginner sort out these black bogies, and direct comparison is the only way. We have on the page two drongoes, one flycatcher and one cuckooshrike, and sooner or later you are going to meet them in the flesh. The two drongoes and the flycatcher are all still-hunters, perching conspicuously and darting out after some passing insect. The cuckooshrike feeds within the bush canopy and is less conspicuous than the others.

Forktailed Drongo. This common bushveld bird is noisy and aggressive, often chasing birds much larger than itself. It is distinctive in having a *markedly forked tail*. In flight its wing feathers appear transparent.

Squaretailed Drongo. A bird of evergreen forest edges and riverine forests. Its tail is more square than the previous species but is also fanned and slightly indented at the end as illustrated. It is also noisy and aggressive towards other birds. Its *eye is ruby-red*, not brown.

Black Flycatcher. A smaller, quieter bird than the drongoes and found in a variety of bushy habitats. Its tail is straight and has a *small indentation at the tip*. In flight its wings also appear transparent.

Black Cuckooshrike male. This bird has a *rounded tail* and may have a yellow shoulder-patch. When the shoulder-patch is absent it can be told by the *orange gape*.

KURRICHANE THRUSH

The name Kurrichane, as in Kurrichane Thrush, and pronounced KURRY-CHARNY, is derived from the former name of the western Transvaal town of Zeerust, originally called Kurrichane after a local chief of that name.

Kurrichane and Olive Thrushes, page 312. Two superficial look-alikes, the Kurrichane a woodland species that enters certain suburbs, the Olive Thrush a forest species that is nevertheless also a common garden bird. Both have yellow-orange beaks and legs, both have orange underparts, but note that the *Kurrichane Thrush has a white belly*. In fact the Kurrichane has distinctly brighter plumage than the Olive Thrush. Whereas the Kurrichane has a bold black malar streak from each corner of its bill, the Olive has a spotted throat. The amount of orange colouring on the underparts of the Olive Thrush is variable; see the fieldguide.

Dull-looking chats, page 320. This page presents two brownish and two greyish chats of closely similar appearance. Unless you live in or visit the Karoo or Namibia, it is not likely that you will meet numbers 1, 3 and 4, as can be seen from the distribution maps in the fieldguide. However, no. 2, the Familiar Chat, is common and widespread around farms and country home-steads, where it is tame. The jizz and behaviour of this bird will serve as a guide for most other chats: it has a fairly upright stance and *frequently flicks its wings*. When you see this action in a robin-like bird you can be sure that you are looking at a chat. Having established that look next at the bird's upper tail pattern and check it against the fieldguide illustrations for a final ID.

Cisticolas. See my remarks about LBJs. Leave them until later.

Prinias. The little prinias (page 358) are fairly easily identified at family level by their long tails that are mostly held aloft and by their familiar 'chip chip chip...' calls. In the more northerly regions the black chest-band of the Blackchested Prinia is suffi-cient to separate it from the otherwise similar Tawnyflanked Prinia, except in winter. At this time, when the birds have reverted to their non-breeding plumage, the black chest-band of the Blackchested Prinia may disappear altogether or be reduced to a small central spot. The clue then is the *yellow wash on the underbody*. Also in the northerly and easterly regions the Drakensberg Prinia, a bird of the Drakensberg escarpment, has yellow underparts from eyebrows to vent, which it wears all year, but it has in addition a *spotted breast*.

In the southerly regions the Karoo Prinia (previously called the Spotted Prinia) and Namaqua Prinia are closely similar but, whereas the Karoo Prinia is *well streaked black on its breast and thighs*, the Namaqua Prinia is only *lightly streaked on its upper breast* and has a tawny wash on its flanks and under-tail coverts.

Flycatchers. Fantailed and Bluegrey Flycatchers, page 362. Although these two are superficially similar they have quite dif-ferent habits. The Fantailed Flycatcher is a highly active leaf-gleaner, always on the move through the mid-stratum of bushveld and woodland, raising and lowering its fanned, white-edged tail while calling continuously. In contrast the Bluegrey Flycatcher is a quiet, unobtrusive species that still-hunts from some low perch.

Spotted and Dusky Flycatchers, page 362. These two quiet, inconspicuous species are a regular cause of confused identity. First remember that the Spotted Flycatcher is a non-breeding summer visitor. Its so-called spots are merely vague smudges on the breast. During the summer it occurs in woodland and in well-wooded suburbia, perching on some low branch, usually below the tree canopy, from where it still-hunts. The resident Dusky Flycatcher, smaller and tubbier than the previous species, has similar dull breast smudges but is duller than the Spotted. It frequents the edges of evergreen indigenous forests, lush riverine woodland and coastal bush; its feeding habits are similar to those of the Spotted Flycatcher.

Mousecoloured, Marico and Chat Flycatchers, pages 362-5. All three are 'wait-and-watch' flycatchers, or still-hunters as we call them: they catch insects by perching conspicuously on the outer branch of a tree, telephone wire or whatever from where they fly to the ground to seize their prey, usually returning to the same perch afterwards. Of the three the Marico is by far the easiest to see and recognise because of its white underparts, visible from afar. It is a mainly westerly bird.

The problem of distinguishing between Mousecoloured and Chat Flycatchers is hypothetical since a glance at the distribution maps will show that their ranges are mutually exclusive: where the one is the other isn't. But if that doesn't convince you you'll find the Mousecoloured (white mice excluded) in broadleafed woodland, never thornveld. The Chat Flycatcher occurs in the western thornveld regions.

Fiscal Flycatcher, page 364, and **Fiscal Shrike,** page 372. This is one of those ID puzzles that can be solved on family beak shape: the flycatcher has a slender bill typical of an insect-eater; the shrike has the stout, hooked bill of a predatory bird. If the beaks cannot be seen their white wing-bars solve the mystery: halfway along the wing in the Fiscal Flycatcher, all the way to the shoulder in the Fiscal Shrike.

Batis flycatchers, page 366. The five batis flycatchers are mostly segregated by their discrete distributions, but the ID of the Cape and Chinspot Batises calls for some guidance. Apart from their different eye colours and plumage markings, which are clearly shown in the fieldguide, their calls and habitat preferences differ. The Cape Batis is a bird of evergreen forest edges, forested kloofs, riverine and coastal bush and well wooded gardens. They occur usually in family groups of about ten birds, occasionally more. They have a variety of calls, a grating 'wee-war-

DID YOU KNOW?

Whitebrowed Sparrow-weavers build their untidy, grass nests in colonies usually on the west side of a thorn tree. Why this should be is not known but it could result in the nests being warmed by the afternoon sun prior to nightfall. A much-repeated camp fire tale has it that a traveller in the bush can check his direction of travel by locating these nests, but be warned, some maverick sparrow-weavers build their nests on any side of the tree except the west!

rawarra...' or 'prrritt, prrritt, prrritt...' and so on. By contrast the Chinspot Batis (named for the rusty chin-spot of the female) is a bird of bushveld and woodland, generally in drier country than the Cape Batis. They occur usually in pairs and have a variety of calls of which the well-known, descending 'three blind mice' or 'choi choi choi' call is most characteristic. See the fieldguide for other calls.

Tchagra shrikes, page 376. The Southern, Threestreaked and Blackcrowned Tchagras are all closely similar in appearance but, provided they can be examined at close range, the Threestreaked and Blackcrowned Tchagras, which share a bushveld habitat, can be seen to have brown and black crowns respectively. The Southern Tchagra also has a brown crown (it is sometimes called the Brownheaded Tchagra) but is not often confused with the other two since its habitat preference and range mostly differ from those of the other two.

The Southern Tchagra spends much of its time feeding on the ground in dense, matted bush, coastal dune forests and montane *Hypericum* scrub. Its range is mostly coastal from about Cape Town northwards to Swaziland and thereafter along the Drakensberg escarpment to the northern Transvaal, where it is uncommon. The usual call of the Southern Tchagra is a stuttering 'trrr-t-t-ttew tew tew tew tew' in descending cadence.

The Threestreaked Tchagra feeds on or close to the ground in bushveld, thornveld and woodland over a wide area, much of its range being shared with the Blackcrowned Tchagra. Its usual call is given in flight when it descends with flickering wings calling a descending 'tew tew tew tew tew tew tew'.

The Blackcrowned Tchagra shares the same habitats and range as the preceding species but avoids the more arid regions. Its call, a well-known bushveld sound, is a ponderous 'CHEER-tcharee, trichi CHEER-tcharoo, cheeroo, cheer-cheercheroo'.

LBJ'S WITH A DIFFERENCE

One day, when you are brave enough to look at LBJ's, you'll see a small, grey-brown, sparrow-like bird with a stout conical beak that shows a yellow rump as it flies away. Will you be able to put a name to it?

In fact the identification will be easy because there are only two sparrow-like birds with yellow rumps, and they are both to be found on pages 438-9 of the fieldguide, in the pale green section. They are the Whitethroated and Blackthroated Canaries. The larger Whitethroated Canary occurs only in the south-western Cape and Namibia, whereas the smaller Blackthroated Canary is common and widespread throughout the region except in the costal districts, and it frequently comes into gardens. Both canaries are good songsters.

Bush shrikes with orange breasts, pages 378-81. Southern Africa has four colourful bush shrikes with yellow underparts, orange breasts and grey heads. They are the Olive, Orangebreasted, Blackfronted and Greyheaded Bush Shrikes. In the colour plates in the fieldguide their different markings and colours are clearly apparent, but in the field confusion frequently reigns. Once again their habitat preferences and calls provide the answers. Two are birds of evergreen forests and two are bushveld birds.

Olive Bush Shrike. This species comes in two colour forms, the cinnamon-breasted (which is more common) and the orange-breasted. It's a bird of *evergreen montane and coastal forests* plus dense riverine and montane *Hypericum* scrub. A secretive bird, heard more often than seen. It forages at all levels from the canopy to the lower stratum. Its calls are varied, always in a descending cadence; 'phwee phwee phwee phwee phwee phwee' or 'tee toy toy toy toy toy' or ' tew tew tew tew tew tew'.

Blackfronted Bush Shrike. Another species of *montane and lowland evergreen forests* where it feeds mainly in the canopy. Not often seen but may be heard calling, especially during summer. The most common call note is a simple 'oo-poo', the second note higher than the first, like 'doh-me' in the tonic sol-fa scale.

Orangebreasted Bush Shrike. This is a *bushveld and woodland species* also occurring in riverine and coastal thickets. It feeds in the mid-stratum and is not particularly secretive. When calling it is easily located by its characteristic 'poo poo poo poooo' or 'pipit-eeez, pipit-eeez' notes.

Greyheaded Bush Shrike. Another bird of *bushveld, woodland and riverine thickets* where it forages at all levels. Easily overlooked when not calling despite its being larger than the previous three species. The usual call is a haunting, drawn-out 'hooooooooooooop' or 'hooooooooooo-up'.

Wattled Starling, page 382. While the headgear of the breeding male Wattled Starling appears unforgettable comparatively few males in a breeding flock have these adornments; some may have the throat wattles and lack those on the head. More commonly females and non-breeding males have neither and are then rather plain, and entire flocks at certain times of the year are made up of such birds.

Glossy starlings. This group is made up of dark-eyed species and orange-eyed ones, and their specific identification causes problems even to fairly experienced birders. Let's look at the dark-eyed ones first.

Longtailed and Burchell's Glossy Starlings, page 384. The Longtailed is a bird of fairly dry conditions and in some regions is confined to Mopane woodland whereas in others it appears to be equally at home away from Mopane. Its body is slimmer than that of Burchell's and its *tail much longer and graduated*, the outer tail feathers being short and becoming progressively longer towards the centre. Burchell's, a bird of well-developed woodland, has a heavier body and comparatively longer legs, imparting a lanky jizz. In good light Burchell's can be seen to have a *black mask extending from its bill to its ear coverts*.

Blue-eared and Cape Glossy Starlings, page 386. More lookalikes! The two blue-eared glossies and the Cape Glossy can largely be separated on distribution but not entirely. While the two blue-eareds have a northerly distribution the Cape covers much of southern Africa but not Mozambique. Most confusion is caused in the north-eastern Transvaal, especially in the

THOSE DARNED WEAVERS

Weavers that strip leaves from a branch prior to building a nest on it are a cause for much consternation among garden-proud urban dwellers, and I get many frantic telephone calls asking for a solution. If you are worried unduly by the sight of falling leaves a weaver can usually be dissuaded in the early stages by tossing sand or fine gravel at it whenever it returns to the tree. Now this, I realise, takes time (two or three days) and perseverance (get a child to do it), but it does work; the weaver will eventually give up and move next door, so don't tell your neighbour how you do it.

Why do weavers strip leaves? Not, contrary to popular belief, to prevent snakes from reaching the nest. Any self respecting snake is able to traverse a bare branch and reach a nest with ease. Let's take as an example the Masked Weaver, the most widespread and well known of the family. The male, having built a nest at the end of a branch, hangs beneath it with fluttering wings and fanned tail while making a 'swizzling' sound. This display is his way of attracting a mate to move in and shack up with him. If he were to attempt this while concealed by leaves he might remain a bachelor, so the explanation is exposure; his display must be seen to be successful.

Masked Weavers (and some other weavers too) may build dozens of nests during a season. If a female does not accept a nest the male tears it down and starts again with inexhaustible determination; if she does accept it she will line it with grass heads and leaves. Since the Masked Weaver is a polygamous creature the male will endeavour to have two or three mates at a time and as many as eight successful broods may be reared during a season.

Kruger Park, where the Cape Glossy, the Greater Blue-eared and, to a lesser extent, the Lesser Blue-eared overlap.

For favourable viewing of these starlings good sunlight is almost essential: only then can the dark ear-patches of the blue-eared species be detected. The Greater Blue-eared, which is common in the more northerly rest camps of the Kruger Park and at the Tshokwane picnic site, has royal blue flanks and belly, and distinct black spots at the tips of the wing coverts. The folded wings themselves appear distinctly greenish in contrast to the bluer body. The Lesser Blue-eared Glossy Starling, slightly smaller than the Greater, only enters the extreme north-east of the Kruger Park but is commoner in Zimbabwe. Its colouring is very similar to that of the Greater but its flanks are more magenta in colour. Without direct comparison with its larger cousin its identity can be overlooked.

However, when a flock is made up of immature birds, and this is often the case, its ID is confirmed by the presence of the brownish young birds.

The Cape Glossy Starling has no dark ear-patch, is bluish overall, less glossy than the blue-eareds and, in poor light, can appear blackish. The wing-spots are less conspicuous than in the blue-eareds. In the Kruger Park it is most common in the more southerly regions and can be seen alongside the Greater Blue-eared at Tshokwane.

To complete the picture the Blackbellied Glossy Starling, with its mainly coastal distribution, is a much duller bird and, as its name suggests, has a blackish belly. The Sharptailed Glossy Starling occurs only in the extreme north-west. It has a reddish eye and a graduated tail.

Garden sparrows. The House and Cape Sparrows, page 404-7. The House Sparrow is an introduced species that has now moved into towns, villages and permanent camps throughout southern Africa. Being commensal with humans (which means it relies on the food scraps discarded by humans) it's never far from the kitchen door. The male with its grey cap, black bib and beak is easily recognised, whereas the duller female with its much paler bill and plumage is less easily identified unless with a male. The call is 'chissip' or 'chee-ip'. House sparrows build an untidy nest of dried grasses, wool, feathers and other scraps which is usually placed under the eaves or in thatch.

The Cape Sparrow is an indigenous species and is less widely distributed than the House Sparrow. A common garden bird in many regions, it is also found in farmlands, parks and semi-arid thornveld. Both sexes have rich chestnut colouring on their mantles and similar head markings; that of the male black, that of the female grey. Both sexes have black bills. The call of the Cape Sparrow is 'chirrup' or 'cheep-chereeep'. The nest is placed in a tree and is a bulky, untidy ball of dried grasses, string, wool, paper or plastic scraps with an entrance on one side; the interior is well lined with feathers.

Three masked weavers, page 412. The sparrow-sized Masked, Lesser Masked and Spottedbacked Weavers are often identified as one species on the basis of the conspicuous yellow males, whereas in fact they are three distinct, similar looking species. The clues to the identities of the males lie in the extent of the black mask and their eye colours.

The Masked Weaver has *a red eye* and the *mask extends over its forehead in a narrow band above its beak*. The Lesser Masked Weaver has *pale yellow eyes* and the *mask extends over the top of its head*. The Spottedbacked Weaver has a *red eye* while, in the southern race, *the mask does not extend to the top of its head* but ends just above its eyes, whereas in the northern race the head is entirely black, as illustrated in the fieldguide. A further feature is that the *black throat extends onto the upper breast in a point*.

When weavers are breeding an examination of the nest types will establish the ID of the owners; see pages 414-15.

During the non-breeding period males lose their masks and bright plumages and resemble the females, the beaks of both sexes becoming pinkish-horn in colour. Eye colours remain a good clue while the smaller Lesser Masked Weaver is always less green, more yellow, than the Masked. In the non-breeding Spottedbacked Weaver the white belly is retained while an additional feature is its larger, sharper beak which, at this time, is a pinkish-horn colour.

Cape and Golden Weavers, page 410. These two are slightly larger than a sparrow (16-18 cm). Their ranges only overlap on the northern section of the eastern Cape and Natal coastlines where problems of ID occur. The males of both species have large, black, sharply pointed beaks. The eyes of the Cape Weaver are *pale yellow to creamy or whitish*, those of the Golden Weaver yellow. The breeding Cape Weaver has a yellow body with a marked suffusion of *brownish-orange over the head and throat; there is a black spot between the eye and bill* (the lores). The upper wings are olive-green. When not breeding the male resembles the female. The male Golden Weaver in breeding plumage is predominantly golden-yellow, paler on the underparts, with a *soft suffusion of orange on the throat and upper breast* (check against the Brownthroated Weaver, below). The yellow-green of the upperparts extends over the crown. The female is similar to the breeding male, perhaps a little paler while, in the non-breeding season, both sexes have pinkish-horn bills.

Brownthroated Weaver, page 410. When breeding the male of this small weaver is entirely golden-yellow with *a clearly defined* brown patch from eyes to throat; the eyes are reddish-brown, the bill black. When not breeding it resembles the female, having greener upperparts and a pale beak, and lacking the brown throat-patch.

Widows and whydahs. There has long been much confusion in the naming of members of these two families, possibly brought about by the fact that males of both may have long tails, but the fact is that even today many bird books confuse the names. A simple rule to remember is that widowbirds and the related bishops (pages 416-19) breed in the normal way and raise their own young. Whydahs and the related widowfinches, on the other hand, are brood parasites: like cuckoos they lay their eggs in the nest of a host species.

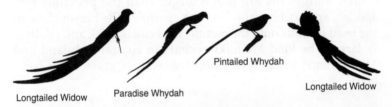

Pintailed Whydah

Longtailed Widow

Longtailed Widow   Paradise Whydah

Widows or whydahs?

Firefinches, page 422. The three red members of the waxbill family that are called firefinches (Redbilled, Bluebilled and Jameson's) call for a little ID guidance. These little birds are normally seen in small flocks, often with other waxbills, and they feed on the ground on ungrassed patches and footpaths, usually in thornveld. When disturbed the flock flies into a nearby bush. First check the distribution maps to see which are in your area. Then note that the female Redbilled Firefinch is predominantly grey-brown in colour and, in a flock where both sexes are present, their identity is certain. Both sexes of the Bluebilled Firefinch (the bills of this and the next species are about identical) are darker than the others, the upperparts are greyish-brown and this extends to the crown (except in Zimbabwe birds). The Jameson's Firefinch male is more rose-red than the others, this colour also suffusing its upperparts so that there is little difference between the colour of the body and the crown and mantle. The female is a little pinker, with a rusty suffusion on the upperparts and flanks.

Mannikins, page 430. These very small, black-headed little birds are described in my fieldguide as very common (Bronze Mannikin), fairly common (Redbacked Mannikin) and uncommon (Pied Mannikin). Their heavy, conical beaks indicate that they are seed-eaters; in fact they feed mostly on grass seeds.

Bronze Mannikins are very common in our coastal regions, rather less common inland where they frequent a variety of habitats. Their small size, two-coloured beak and green-bronze shoulder feathers are diagnostic. Bronze Mannikins are found in flocks.

Redbacked Mannikins, as their name suggests, have much brighter, red-brown upperparts and more extensive black on the head and upper breast; their beaks are whitish or pale grey. Redbacks occur in eastern bushveld and coastal dune forests.

Pied Mannikins are much larger than the previous two species, approaching the size of a sparrow. The bluish-black of the head extends onto the mantle, the beak is black and relatively large. The Pied Mannikin occurs in coastal Zululand and Mozambique where it feeds on the seeds of grasses and bamboo.

LBJs with white eyebrows. The Streakyheaded Canary (page 438) and the Yellowthroated Sparrow (page 404) are the only two LBJs with very bold, white eyebrows. Both are normal sparrow size, the Streakyheaded Canary with distinctive black and white streaks on its crown plus a heavy, conical beak, the Yellowthroated Sparrow with (sometimes) a small, pale yellow spot on its throat. If the throat-spot is absent note the less heavy bill and lack of head-streaks.

REFERENCES

Birdlife in Southern Africa.
K. Newman (ed), 1980. Macmillan South Africa.

Roberts' Birds of Southern Africa.
Gordon Lindsay Maclean (ed) 1985. Trustees of the John Voelcker Bird Book Fund, Cape Town.

Southern African Bird Names Explained.
Charles Clinning, 1989. Southern African Ornithological Society

USEFUL NAMES AND ADDRESSES

Various organisations run birding courses, birding trips and safaris.
The following bird clubs and commercial companies will be able to
tell you what is available in your area.

Cape Bird Club:
PO Box 5022, Cape Town 8000

Eastern Cape Bird Society:
PO Box 27454, Greenacres,
Port Elizabeth 6057

Goldfields Bird Club:
PO Box 580, Virginia 9430

Lowveld Bird Club:
PO Box 4113, Nelspruit 1200

Namibia Bird Club:
PO Box 67, Windhoek, Namibia

Natal Bird Club:
PO Box 1218, Durban 4000

Natal Midlands Bird Club:
PO Box 2772,
Pietermaritzburg 3200

North-eastern Bird Club:
PO Box 6007, Pietersburg 0750

**Northern Transvaal
Ornithological Society:**
PO Box 4158, Pretoria 0001

**Orange Free State
Ornithological Society:**
PO Box 6614, Bloemfontein 9300

Rand Barbets Bird Club:
135 Oxford Road,
Saxonwold 2193

Sandton Bird Club:
PO Box 650890, Benmore 2010

Vaal Reefs Bird Club:
PO Box 5129, Vaal Reefs 2621

Wesvaal Bird Club:
PO Box 2413,
Potchefstroom 2520

Witwatersrand Bird Club:
PO Box 72091, Parkview,
Johannesburg, 2122

or

**Southern African
Ornithological Society**
PO Box 87234,
Houghton, Johannesburg, 2041
Tel (011) 888 4147

Monty Brett Bird Courses:
*bird identification courses in all
major centres, beginners courses
and specialised refresher courses for
the more advanced bird-watcher*
PO Box 650727,
Benmore, 2010
Tel (011) 783 6629
Fax (011) 783 6535

Monty Brett Birding Safaris:
*both local and international under
expert guidance*
PO Box 651171,
Benmore, 2010
Tel (011) 783 6629
Fax (011) 783 6535

Wilderness Safaris:
*bird-watching safaris under the
guidance of experienced
ornithologists to Botswana,
Namibia, Zimbabwe and Malawi*
PO Box 651171,
Benmore, 2010
Tel (011) 884 1458
Fax (011) 883 6255

BIRDING JARGON

Acacia:

deciduous trees of the genus *Acacia*. In Africa these are thorny, with bipinnately compound leaves (each leaf is again divided into small leaflets) and small, powderpuff-like or elongated flowers.

Accipiter:

sparrowhawks and goshawks. Long-tailed, short-winged raptors with long, unfeathered legs and long toes. They specialise in catching small birds (or small mammals in the larger species) in swift pursuit from a standing start.

Aggregation:

a gathering (of birds) brought about by some common interest such as a temporary food availability, after which individuals disperse separately.

Brood parasite:

birds which deposit their eggs in the nest of another species, e.g. cuckoos, honeyguides, whydahs, etc.

Crepuscular:

active at dusk. When applied to birds, it usually infers that they are active in the half-light hours, dawn and dusk.

Decurved:

downward-curved.

Delta:

a river mouth with several diverging branches which form a triangle. In the context of the fieldguide, usually refers to the inland delta of the Okavango River drainage system (also known as the Okavango Swamps) in northern Botswana.

Dispersal:

a more or less random centrifugal movement away from a locality.

Display:

a term used to denote actions that have become specialised in the course of evolution: threat display, courtship display, social displays, etc.

Egg-dumping:

the habit among secondary females in such social species as the ostrich, guineafowls and others, of laying their eggs in the nest of another female of the same species, usually the dominant female in a flock. Also refers to random egg-laying in places other than nests by immature or unmated hens of any species.

Endemic:

refers to species found only in a specific region or country.

Estuary:

the tidal mouth of a large river, an important feeding area for many water-associated birds because of its food-rich mud-flats and floodplains.

Escarpment:	the long steep face of a plateau. In Southern Africa usually refers to the eastern escarpment which forms the edge of the inland plateau or highveld.
Ethiopian Region:	old name of Africa south of the Palaearctic Region, now replaced by the term Afrotropical Region.
Falcon:	small, swift-flying raptors with pointed wings; they specialise in catching flying birds by means of a rapid descent from above, known as a `stoop'.
Flats:	level grassland.
Fledgling:	a young bird that has recently acquired its first feathers.
Flock:	a group of birds that moves as a more or less cohesive unit.
Floodplain:	grassland, especially that adjacent to estuaries, which becomes inundated from river spillage.
Gamebird:	an outdated term used by hunters. Refers to ducks, geese, pheasants, partridges, guineafowls and others. In the past bustards were included in this category.
Graduated tail:	a tail in which the central feathers are the longest and all others progressively shorter, the outermost being shortest.
Gregarious:	living in flocks or communities.
I.D.:	identify.
Immature:	in the context of the fieldguide, refers to any young bird beyond the nestling stage.
Intra-Africa migrant:	birds that migrate regularly within the African continent.
Irruptive:	an irregular migration into a new area, often brought about by unfavourable conditions in the normal range of a species, and usually of a temporary nature.
Jizz:	the general impression of a bird; its family characteristics.
Juvenile:	young bird below sub-adult stage.
Kloof:	a cleft or valley, usually with steeply inclined or rocky sides, often well-wooded.
Koppie:	a small hill, often with a rocky summit.
Lagoon:	a stretch of salt water separated from the sea by a low sandbank.

LBJ: abbreviation of Little Brown Job. An apparently featureless small brown bird that is difficult to identify.

Leaf-gleaner: a bird that seeks insects from the leaves in a tree canopy.

Life-list: the total list of birds identified in one's life.

Littoral: the region of land lying along the sea shore.

Local movement: a mass movement, not necessarily regular, within a comparatively small area.

Macchia: a natural habitat occurring in the south-eastern and south-western coastal regions of the Cape Province: a Mediterranean-type scrub composed of Proteas, Ericas and legumes among other plants.

Mangrove: a forest of mainly trees of the family Rhizophoraceae which grows in tidal estuaries. The trees produce air roots, which protrude upwards from the mud.

Melanistic: darkness of plumage colour resulting from abnormal development of black pigmentation.

Migration: a regular movement of birds (or other animals) between two alternative regions inhabited by them at different times of the year, one region in which they breed and the other region used by them when not breeding.

Miombo: broadleafed woodland in which trees of the genus *Brachystegia* dominate; common in Zimbabwe.

Mistbelt: the eastern region of southern Africa at 900-1350 m above sea level (otherwise known as the escarpment) where the rainfall is between 900 and 1150 mm per annum and the conditions are frequently misty during easterly maritime winds; of mostly hilly or montane grassland with isolated forest patches and, these days, with extensive exotic plantations.

Monoculture: regions extensively planted with one crop, e.g. sugarcane.

Montane: mountainous country.

Mopane: a broadleafed, deciduous tree, *Colophospermum mopane*. In some regions remains as a smallish bush, in other regions grows to a height of *c*. 12 m. Leaves are rounded, heart-shaped and reddish when young.

Morph: an alternative but permanent plumage colour.

Nomad: a species with no fixed territory when not breeding.

Palaearctic Region: the northern hemisphere, incorporating North Africa, Europe, Scandinavia and Asia.

Pan (or flood-pan): a natural depression which fills with water as the result of rainfall or river spillage.

Parkland: regions of woodland with well-spaced trees, little secondary growth and a grassy groundcover.

Passerine: birds that habitually sing or call and that have `normal' feet, with three toes facing forward and one facing backward; excludes birds with webbed, lobed, or zygodactylous feet.

Pectoral: the breast region; in birds especially the lateral breast regions.

Pelagic seabird: a bird of the open seas as opposed to one which roosts or breeds on mainland shores.

Range expansion: the process in which a species increases its breeding range; a spread into regions not previously occupied.

Raptor: a bird of prey; one which hunts and kills other animals for food.

Rectrices: the main tail feathers of a bird (Rectrix in the singular).

Recurved bill: a bill that bends upwards, e.g. Avocet.

Remiges: the primary and secondary wing feathers of a bird (Remex in the singular).

Riparian: of or on riverbanks.

Sexual dimorphism: differences in appearance between male and female of a species.

Soft parts: a bird's bill, legs and feet, eye-surround and bare facial skin if present.

Speculum: a patch of iridescent colour on the wings of some birds, notably ducks.

Still-hunt: watching for prey (usually on the ground) while perched.

Sub-adult: a young bird in the final stages of immaturity.

Subantarctic: the southern oceans between 45°S and the Antarctic Circle.

Sub-song: a bird song of lower than normal pitch, sometimes of longer than normal duration.

Scrub: brushwood or stunted bushes.

Tail-streamer:	elongated tail-feathers, often the central or outer feathers.
Thicket:	a number of shrubs or trees growing very close together.
Twitcher:	one who goes to extreme lengths to extend his/her life-list.
Understorey:	refers to the lowest stratum in (usually) forest or woodland: secondary growth consisting of young trees, small bushes and annual plants.
Upland:	refers to high altitude regions below that of montane.
Vlei:	a marshy area, usually in grassland.
Watercourse:	the dry course of a river that flows only during good rains.
Waterhole:	any natural or man-made waterpoint used by animals for drinking.
Zygodactyl:	feet which, in certain non-passerine birds, have two toes directed forward and two backward: cuckoos, barbets, woodpeckers, honeyguides and others.

INDEX